SOCIAL WORK
AS ART

SOCIAL WORK AS ART

Making sense for Good Practice

HUGH ENGLAND

School of Cultural and Community Studies,
University of Sussex

LONDON
ALLEN & UNWIN
Boston   Sydney

© H. England, 1986

Allen & Unwin (Publishers) Ltd,
40 Museum Street, London WC1A 1LU, UK

Allen & Unwin (Publishers) Ltd,
Park Lane, Hemel Hempstead, Herts HP2 4TE, UK

Allen & Unwin, Inc.,
8 Winchester Place, Winchester, Mass. 01890, USA

Allen & Unwin (Australia) Ltd,
8 Napier Street, North Sydney, NSW 2060, Australia

First published in 1986

British Library Cataloguing in Publication Data

England, Hugh
    Social work as art: making sense for good practice
    1. Social service
    I. Title
361.3 HV40
ISBN 0–04–360063–8
ISBN 0–04–360064–6 Pbk

Library of Congress Cataloging-in-Publication Data

England, Hugh.
    Social work as art
Bibliography: p.
Includes index
    1. Social service. 2. Social case work. 3. Social workers. I. Title.
HV40.E54 1986 361.3 85–15739
ISBN 0–04–360063–8 (alk. paper)
ISBN 0–04–360064–6 (pbk.: alk. paper)

Set in 10 on 11 point Sabon by
Computape (Pickering) Ltd, North Yorkshire
and printed in Great Britain by
Biddles Limited, Guildford, Surrey

Contents

Acknowledgements

Much of this book is rooted in ideas given to me over the years by colleagues at the University of Sussex, although they may be surprised at the direction in which these ideas have been taken. During the preparation of the book many people have shown an enthusiastic interest and I am grateful for numerous discussions which gave me real encouragement. I have been helped in particular by Veronica Wood and Stuart Laing, who consistently gave me useful comments and suggestions, and by Yvonne Wood, who worked carefully and thoughtfully on the typescript.

I am especially indebted to the authors of the three accounts of practice for their co-operation and for the permission they have given me to use their work.

Acknowledgement is also due to Chatto & Windus/The Hogarth Press and Columbia University Press for permission to reproduce extracts from *The Long Revolution* by Raymond Williams, and to Gower Publishing Co. Ltd., for extracts from *Understanding and the Human Sciences* by H. P. Rickman, published by Heinemann Education Books.

1

Introduction:
A Sense of the
Possible Glory

Times continue to be difficult for social work. The difficulties are familiar, but they have lately appeared in particularly virulent forms – ridicule and hostility for lack of purpose, method and effect, and eventually a government initiated inquiry into the 'role and tasks' of the social worker (the 'Barclay Report', the National Institute for Social Work (NISW), 1982). This suspicion of social work has been increased by the current unprecedented concern of the public authorities to trim priorities and seek economic effectiveness. Recent changes offer no immediate comfort; indeed, the major change, the reorganization of many social services consequent upon the Seebohm Report (Home Office, 1968), has had an effect upon social work which now seems to some a cure worse than the ill it removed. Nonetheless, for all its present troubles, social work is as a result of these changes much more accessible to clarification. It is therefore no coincidence that some clarity *has* emerged over this same period. One area of real gain has been the development of frameworks for analysing practice which are very much more plausible constructs than earlier models; social workers may not sigh with relief at the appearance of, for example, the task-centred approach to social work, but such developments are helping social work acquire the means to be much clearer about its real character and practice.

This need to be clear is a desperately important matter. It is also a matter of considerable complexity. It is, I will suggest, a complexity which is widely felt but little appreciated – as if social workers are acutely aware of the constant difficulty they have in explaining what they do (even, I believe, to themselves), and of the embarrassment – and worse – associated with their constant search for an adequate description. Yet it is as if, despite this constant difficulty, they see no choice but to pursue the search by a now well-worn cycle of working parties, reports and investigations – a cycle which at best can offer only a description of and not a reason for the nature of the social worker's practice. In themselves, of course, these approaches have been helpful; they have made clear some aspects of social work. But they are not sufficient; social work is more than a description of the general problems of the client and of the procedures and organization which are relevant to these problems. Some recent developments in social work theory have helped describe this 'more'; this book is intended to take one further step towards its clarification.

If I imagine social work as an entity I see it as a curiously puzzled and confused body. There are parts rushing off in all directions and sometimes falling over each other in the process. They are rushing to be busy and to be engaged, for to be busy and engaged is to feel assured that something worthwhile and important is being done – and social workers deal with problems that cannot humanely be neglected. But busy doing what? For to be busy is also often to be too busy to think and at times of confusion this state has its advantages – I recall one of my earliest social work colleagues explaining only half jokingly that he strove to preserve the size of his enormous workload because it was then much more difficult for him to be held responsible for its organization. The current 'organizational malaise' in social work has something of this quality; it may be that the agencies are organized in a way which makes social work difficult (which is the report of so many practitioners) in part because of confusion about the nature of the social work service which it is one of their principal responsibilities to deliver. The complex economic and administrative tasks faced by the agencies are familiar, but these sometimes obscure the fact that one of the most difficult burdens the agencies carry is the uncertainty of the nature of social work itself.

This is an old and well-worn problem. Barbara Wootton was, long ago, very funny about the apparent 'absurdity' of social work's pretensions. Writing about the report of the Younghusband Working Party on social work in health and welfare services (Ministry of Health, 1959), she noted a

> picture of the social worker as professionally competent to resolve the problems which have defeated the human race since the day of Adam and Eve – as in the Committee's endorsement of the definition of casework as a 'personal service provided by qualified workers for individuals who require skilled assistance in resolving some material, emotional or character problem'. If these skills really exist surely they are wasted upon obscure members of the British working classes; would not the caseworkers do better to get their hands on some of our world's rulers? (Wootton, 1959)

Wootton was right; right, that is, in some measure. Her sceptical humour emphasized one strand of the problem for the social worker: how does he know that he is being helpful, that his skills 'really exist'? There has been no shortage of subsequent activity in the areas of practice Wootton preferred – of social workers seeking to guide their clients about the maze of welfare rules and regulations. For if to be busy is to feel useful, to be busy on 'measurable' activities – getting benefits, clarifying applications – is to be busy on matters which can be shown to be useful. And for some workers this certainly eases the puzzled feeling and the confusion; for it is as much necessary for the mental health of social workers as for that of their clients to *know* that their efforts are worthwhile, and their morale, their mental health, has suffered because it has not been clear to them or to others that they have been useful.

There is of course no question that such matters as social security benefit and entitlement are matters of considerable importance – of a more fundamental importance than social work itself. But such matters are not social work ones; it is, for example, a nonsense for social work to dally and tinker on the margins of an income maintenance advisory service. It is evident that there is need for such services; it is evident that the delivery of such services requires considerable knowledge; but it is by no means evident why social work should provide them. It does so only at the cost of its principal role.

The nature of that principal role, while still subject to obvious confusion and challenge, is in fact rather more clear than is sometimes evident in discussion. There is a striking consistency and persistence in descriptions of social work – rather as if the 'confused and puzzled body' was continually banging its head against the wall even when critics kind and stern have suggested stopping. But why is the debate about the nature of social work so persistent? And so persistent in the face of adversity? And so consistent, making the same contentious claims when they have already been the subject of ridicule? In any new review of the nature of social work, the persistence of the need for review and its consistent content ought themselves to become factors to be explained. It seems reasonable to conclude that many contentious descriptions of social work, challenged because they are grandiose, vague and even mystical, are maintained because they speak in some profound way to the knowledge and experience of their authors. Certainly social workers seem unrepentant many years after Wootton's earlier scorn; consider the British Association of Social Workers' description of *The Social Work Task*: 'Social work is the purposeful and ethical application of personal skills in interpersonal relationships directed towards enhancing the personal and social functioning of an individual, family, group or neighbourhood' (BASW, 1977). Yet in the different context of the 1970s and 1980s, criticism of such claims carries political and administrative implications; an article by Mary Manning (1980) on medical attitudes to social work notes not only the sceptical reception of this description, but the British Medical Association's subsequent policy of seeking to transfer control of social services to 'competent medical personnel'. Social work persists in its description, but the criticism loses none of its edge.

In fact, such descriptions are not satisfactory; in some ways, they merit the scorn that they attract and the Barclay Report was rightly wary of them. But some significant conviction must encourage social workers to adhere to such description despite attack; and some problem must prevent them finding a better path to articulate the description. Sane people (and good social workers are very sane, despite the impediments to their professional morale) do not keep banging their heads against the wall without good cause. Good social workers *know*, through their experience, the value of their helping work with clients. That value cannot be abandoned, so a way through the wall must be found; as there is no other route in sight, they must keep banging at the wall until the way is forced. The situation points to one of those gaps between the head and the heart, between understanding and experience, to which social workers so often refer. Their inability to explain and handle this gap is the cause of their dilemma; their inability to find intelligible ways of communicating their experience to their critics means that they can only keep repeating their claims even though they are not heard – indeed, even though they cannot be heard. It is in fact impossible for them to be heard because the familiar structure of debate about the nature of social work precludes its proper discussion and description. The terms employed by the critics of social work demand a 'materialist' reply, a reply about externally measurable procedures and effects. And, since these are the terms of so much conventional debate, can this be unreasonable? Social workers are compelled by their experience to make some reply, for they know social work is too important to be abandoned. But social workers are compelled by their culture to reply using a certain language and certain concepts, for these are the 'givens' of conventional discussion. These two, however – the available experience and the available language – do not meet. Neither do they change. It is for this reason that social work moves around its debilitating treadmill.

Some things do change; the generic reorganization of social work agencies, and the development of models of helping which match more closely the experience of worker and client have helped considerably to clarify the nature of the role of the social worker. But they are not sufficient. They help bring more clearly into focus that there *is* an important experience of helping and that its nature is uncertain. It is this nature which must be clarified as the next stage in the proper establishment of social work. Without such clarification social workers cannot be articulate about their work; in particular, they cannot deal with the recurring accusation that their professional claims are absurd and grandiose, and that their work is invalid because it is subjective and thus precludes evaluation. This 'experience' of helping will prove to have specific theoretical implications; its nature throws light upon the 'bogey' word of social work theory – integration. This term has posed so many problems that some critics have in effect advocated its abolition; yet social work must find a way of explaining two processes of integration if it is to outline any plausible *modus operandi* – it must better understand the processes whereby social workers integrate their knowledge and whereby they integrate theory and practice. It is this development which will be the crucial step towards the establishment of any real 'practice theory' in social work and thus of any real scope for the evaluation of social work practice.

These difficulties lie at the very heart of social work, which is why they have posed such a constant obstacle. It is simply not possible to consider social work without opening them up for discussion and inquiry. But they are not *just* difficulties, for otherwise why should not the body social work decamp, leave the wall behind and set up shop lock, stock and barrel in the income maintenance department, where role, clear purpose and ontological security would be available? Is it essential to this 'experience' of social work that such apparently grandiose claims are made for it? The body social work seems to think that it is; it has responded rather apologetically to the scepticism with which its grand aspirations are greeted, acknowledging not only that it is hard to be precise about its work but that it *should* be precise and that it will try harder to be so in future, but it has not rejected them. Indeed, it should try harder to be precise; social workers have not developed any adequate tradition of intellectual scrutiny and criticism, and their thinking – in the job and in writing – is often lazy. But this inertia is itself attributable to the central confusion; the body social work is not clear why it cannot readily think out the practice it will not abandon, although experience and time imply it cannot do so. Social work therefore comes to be seen as an activity which cannot bear critical scrutiny. It is a fundamental strain for social work that it must persistently strive for a certainty that is in fact inherently unattainable.

It is evident that no material certainty will be possible if social work is a matter of 'personal skills in interpersonal relationships directed towards enhancing ... personal and social functioning'. Yet the real strength of social work is reflected in such claims (despite the horrors of the wording); what social workers know – as, at one level, do we all – is that our experience of the world is underpinned by just such grand, complex compositions. The source of social work's potential strength, and of the conviction of its proponents, is the very fact that it does *not* separate the world experienced by those in need of help into component elements. Such experience is always a complex, composite experience, it is always a unique synthesis; yet it cannot be impossible to construct such a synthesis, because the client – and everyone – does so all the time. The strength of the able worker lies in his ability accurately to join the client in the construction and experience of this synthesis. It is only through such sharing that people sometimes say to others (and should say most often to social workers) 'you seem to understand' – and we know that to be understood by others is a necessary and a therapeutic experience.

There is no fundamental sense, then in which these maligned definitions of social work are wrong, and no fundamental sense in which they have failed to achieve an available precision. At worst it might be said that they are sometimes prosaic and unsubtle in their language, and naive in anticipating acceptance without explanation of their vagueness. Indeed, far from being wrong, their breadth and scope contains the richness from which social work should draw its substantial creative strength. For in making its apology, the body social work has not only failed to dignify and substantiate its own practice; it has also failed to make any significant social contribution beyond its own boundaries. Yet it lies clearly within social work's grasp to do so – indeed it is a function it may *have* to fulfil. It is necessary to mental, and thus to social, well-being that there exist cultural institutions which affirm the value of experience, of what is sometimes called 'the whole man'. In a society which relies increasingly upon the use of formal institutions, only those of social work and education seem placed to take on this role, and of these only social work seems able to give central place to issues of coping and thus of 'learning for maturity'. So the scale of the operation in social work is its rationale; it need not be grandoise, but it should be grand.

The difference between those two terms will lie in the understanding and the attitude of the body social work. It is partly a matter of perception, partly of acceptance – both terms already in the social work vocabulary. It will be a central strand of the following discussion that perception can be consciously altered and extended, indeed that such a process is the very stuff of social work. I hope that the discussion will contribute one nudge towards shifting the perception that the body social work has of itself, so that we may move, in time, towards a better understanding of the work we do. But if my argument is plausible, and some part of social work is a little better understood, it will also be seen that there can never be an adequate material description of social work, and that this is a necessary corollary of the very elements which make up social work's strength. In a world banging the drum for precision it will need 'acceptance' to live with this uncertainty. Yet social work really has no choice; it is an integral part of its own faith and rationale, its own logic, that it must explore and accept this perspective – in some other form if not in this present one.

The argument presented here is not a new argument; it will be evident at various points in the subsequent discussion that other writers have felt it necessary to approach this area, but also that often they have then been uncertain how to proceed. It will in any case, by its nature, prove an argument which must be repeatedly rehearsed and explored if social work is to become clearer about its practice, about the way it works. It will be a gain though if social workers can find within these chapters a description which comes a little nearer their own experience, and if the argument can therefore contribute towards a more optimistic tone in future discussion in social work. Noel and Rita Timms (1977) are amongst those whose writing has already touched upon these themes; referring to the related issue of the diversity of social work, they wrote that social work's 'boundaries are loosely drawn and often permeable ... This looseness constitutes one of the major challenges, if not one of the glories.' There is no doubt about the size of the challenge; I hope that there will be no doubt that it is also a matter for glory.

PART 1

The Problem
of the
Use of Self

2

Core Concepts:
Coping and Meaning

THE NEED FOR A COMMON THEORETICAL BASE

It is notoriously difficult to find out what social workers *do*. To ask them is to invite vague replies such as 'visit people in need', 'help people' or even 'talk to people'. To survey them is to note their presence in diverse settings and their contact with diverse groups – social workers are well established in court settings and in prisons in their work with offenders, and in hospitals in their work with physically and mentally ill people, and their work with children, families and old people largely occupies the resources of local authority area offices and residential settings. Social workers are also on the move; they are increasingly present in other spheres, such as educational settings and general practice health clinics. It may not be possible to say what social work is, but clearly it is substantial and pervasive.

The implausibilty of this situation has become increasingly evident. Social workers entered the current period of financial stringency already on the defensive after long bouts of ideological skirmish: their principal agencies, in the local authorities, were achieved only after wresting their component units from other established groups; their major responsibility for the treatment of young offenders was achieved only against the persistent opposition of the magistracy; and both these battles, and others, continue still. Perhaps most significant, local authority social workers have curried much disfavour, and scepticism, through their conduct of prolonged strikes and social workers have failed to counter considerable (implausible) newspaper criticsm that they should have been able to prevent several incidents of child abuse. At a time when all public service groups are asked to demonstrate their value and effectiveness, social workers have fewer friends than they would wish.

It seems, not surprisingly, that social workers will survive this period; the government-sponsored report on the role and tasks of social workers (National Institute for Social Work, 1982) has concluded that their work is both necessary and necessarily done by a discrete occupational group; its recommendations are about the substance and not the existence of social work services. But this conclusion will not remove the doubt and dispute which has beset social work because, although the report clarifies what social workers do, it does not make clearer how they do it. It was the achievement of the Seebohm Report (Home Office, 1968) to make more publicly intelligible the existence of recurring personal and social issues which underlay the separate problems which were then the responsibility of different agencies. The subsequent development of unified social services has to a degree included the development of more coherent social work services (that the two are not seen to be different is one of the sources of confusion about the nature of social work), and thus helped move towards a position in which the character of social work can be more adequately clarified. But the recognition of recurring social problems was not of itself such clarification; it has not been appreciated – and this is the basic source of confusion – that while attempts to describe common social work problems and procedures are steps in the right direction, they are not a sufficient description of a professional practice. Social work still has no *identified* substantial unity, no grasp of the underlying basis which gives these problems and procedures their similarity. The confusion about the nature of social work must persist until this substantial basis is made clear.

The diversity of people, problems and settings encompassed by social work requires that any definition is inevitably broadly based and couched in general terms, but it is a mistake to think that this generality must be suspect. It is such suspicion, a pervasive cultural suspicion which social work has mostly echoed, which has inhibited social work from both seeing and then exploring the real basis of its character. It is in fact this generality which gives the lie to the character of social work's distinct unity, for that unity lies in that which is common to all social work; the 'human nature' of its clients. But social work – because it must justify itself and debate within a culture which values material precision – finds little comfort or even plausibility in any concept of 'human nature'; it hardly appears fertile ground for definition. But this appearance reflects these cultural values; it is these cultural priorities, not any inherent absolute, which restrict debate to certain modes of intellectual approach. Social work, fumbling for identity, finds itself debating within the general confines of the scientific wisdom; yet this is only one of the significant intellectual traditions and social work, it will be seen, cannot be properly located within it.

It will require something of an intellectual journey before the utility of the concept 'human nature' will be evident. Its enunci-ation at this stage serves to identify the necessary terms of a debate about social work. Social work may not be offered to the 'world's rulers', as Wootton jibed, but its substance is necessarily as pertinent to them as to all persons. Social work's root concepts are necessarily universal, the concepts of human experience. Yet social workers have been markedly wary of acknowledging them; they are by and large concepts which have been recognized as professionally relevant by social workers, but always in passing or with diffidence, rather than with the enthusiastic celebration which will give social work its necessary foundation.

COPING

There is no superficial uniformity in either the groups of people with whom social workers work or the settings in which they work; nor uniformity in the material or practical help which they may give to their clients. There is nonetheless a 'common base' in the needs to which social workers respond, one of which has been outlined in Harriet Bartlett's curiously neglected book, *The Common Base of Social Work Practice* (1970); that common base is 'coping'. Social workers work not with those people who have problems but with those people who have difficulty coping with their problems. Bartlett discusses the term in the context of 'social functioning' and thus grasps the necessary relativity of the need for social work help; all coping is a function of the interaction between available subjective resources and external resources, both social and material. The relativity of the concept explains the 'selection' of the social worker's clients; social workers do not, for example, help all old or all poor people, but only those who cannot cope. Similarly, social workers may focus upon either the subjective or external resources of their clients, they may offer counselling or material help, according to their judgement of the balance of the 'coping equation'. Social workers constantly make judgements about their clients' coping capacity and how this may best be improved.

It is evident that the social worker as counsellor is concerned with improving his clients' coping capacity; it is not always, apparently, so evident that this is also necessarily the focus of more 'active' social work, when the worker seeks to fulfil tasks or supply material aid for his clients. Yet this must be so, and it is important that this point be clear. The social worker supplies no material or practical service impersonally, independent of his assessment of the client's subjective resources. The diversity and the subsidiary character of such aid both preclude it constituting the primary rationale for social work activity. Its diversity *implicitly* precludes it; social workers might be competent in one, or even a few, fields of material knowledge (for example, income maintenance, housing or health) but the very range of possible 'specialisms' makes it evident that these are not the identifying character of the common social work base. Social workers should, perhaps, 'specialize', but any such specialism is clearly subsidiary to their principal concern, serving only as its context. This in turn suggests the subsidiary character of material aid. The social worker may agree to supply material aid, but it is not a condition of his work that he does so; rather it is a possible element within it. The aid is not routinely or uniformly available; if it were then social workers would only be the administrators of impersonal service. Its discretionary use makes it always only one means to a broader end.

The social worker is always concerned with the delivery of personal service. His work with clients is never only a matter of uniform or bureaucratic procedure, and in as much as social workers may sometimes be required just to fulfil such procedures, they abandon their social work role and become 'only' agents of a bureaucracy; the role makes no reference to a common focus shared with other social workers. But in as much as the worker elects to supply material or practical aid to promote the personal coping capacity of his clients, to promote the balanced inter-action of the clients' subjective and external resources, then the worker uses this aid as a result of his assessment of that coping capacity and it is this assessment that distinguishes his work. If the material or practical aid could be supplied without need for other help it would be impersonal service; in as much as help is needed to apply for or supply the aid, then a social work element enters the procedure. The social worker's help is *never* a matter only of uniform provision; it is always a result of judgement about unique circumstances.

This emphasis upon coping capacity is the initial distinguishing feature of all social work; it underlies not only the counselling or task-centred roles of the worker, but also what the Barclay Report (NISW, 1982) described as 'social policing' and 'social care planning'. An assessment of coping capacity does not necessarily require the active co-operation or agreement of clients; the probation officer may work with offenders who consider their only problem to be their duty to keep contact with the probation officer, but this does not preclude (though it will impede) his assessment of their ability to cope and his attempts to influence it – an assessment in which 'coping' will be defined to include an explicit assessment of the likelihood of avoiding further offences. Similarly 'social care planning' relies upon the assessment of coping capacity; social workers may be asked to consider the future welfare of individuals or groups (even groups of people known only by their membership of a particular 'population', for example, old people in residential care) and such consideration will be an assessment of estimated coping capacity. In the same way, the social work role in community development is a facilitative one, distinguished from explicit organizational or political roles by its emphasis upon the development of coping; and the social work element in residential work is similarly distinguished from the necessary work of routine physical or even routine emotional care.

Coping capacity is thus the principal focus of the social worker, and its identification the first gateway to a better grasp of the unity of social work itself. It does not of itself, however, offer a sufficient purchase. It serves as the first stage of an inquiry about the subject of social work, but it does not explore the nature of that subject. To explore that nature the social worker must know not only that all people's ability to cope is different, but that one necessary element in the determination of that ability must be each person's perceptions. The coping capacity which is the object of social work help can never, by definition, be *only* a matter of material resource or practical provision (though these may feature large in the help provided), but a matter too of the response of each person to his circumstances, of the meaning he gives to his experience. The subject of social work is not only coping, but meaning.

MEANING

A process of 'individualization' has in some social work circles acquired a bad name, as if to attend carefully to individual experience is to allocate responsibility for social ills to the individuals who undergo them. This is an obvious fallacy. On the one hand it overlooks the certainty that, to some extent, people can always personally influence their experience of ill fortune, and that people are sometimes significantly responsible for their experience. How else than by the assertion of individuality can we explain different reactions to similar circumstances and explain the self-destructive scripts that some people evidently enact? On the other hand, it misconstrues the necessary political role of social work. Social work, as we have already seen can never be *only* the pursuit of material or practical help, for it is then not otherwise distinct from other political or organizational activities and it ceases to exist. But such pursuit *is* social work when it remains intimately linked to an understanding of the coping capacity of those who suffer disadvantage, or when it explains the redress of disadvantage not only as a matter of rights but as a matter of the meaning of the experience to those who suffer. Social work may then argue politically that all but the very best endowed would suffer in defined circumstances; it remains social work because of its roots in experience, in meaning. In social work the recognition of the many is always based upon the recognition of the one.

The social worker always has to know not only about the

circumstances of the client's world but also about the client's interpretation of that world; it is this condition that makes social work personal service rather than impersonal assessment for pre-defined material or practical service. Knowledge of such interpretation is not the only knowledge which social workers will require, but other knowledge will vary in varying circumstances; that social workers will need to know about the meaning of experience is the only constant and the only necessary element in all social work accounts. Social work is always about the way in which people see things, and it is a personal service because perception is always unique. Any account of social work must therefore be based upon an account of perception, for social work is based upon the meaning people give to their experience.

The meaning we give to events is necessarily a personal creation. There is in all of us a mechanism which allows us to impose upon the world some order, and to select from the potentially infinite sources of data and stimuli which surround us elements that allow us to experience not undifferentiated chaos but sufficiently organized coherence. This selection and its synthesis is necessarily personal because everyone experiences a different world and reacts differently to the world. But the need to make such a selection and synthesis is not personal; it is a human 'constant', and the adequacy of this created meaning is determined by the extent to which it is accurate and complex enough to be a sufficient expression of personal experience.

This sense of order and coherence enables us to make routine judgements and guides our daily actions with a measure of consistency. Without such consistency our mental health and general well-being is immediately threatened. It is a commonplace that we have to be able to take most aspects of our daily lives for granted; without making assumptions about the response of the ticket clerk, the greeting of our friends or the way in which the kettle will work, we would spend each minute in such a state of uncertainty that our mental and emotional energy would be exhausted. This sense of order is fundamental, a necessary condition of human life.

However, this sense of order is not, as Abercrombie (1969) has shown in *The Anatomy of Judgement*, just a matter of reporting facts; people give the facts their meaning. Abercrombie's work was with medical students who compared their perception of 'objective' data – for example, X-ray pictures – and found that they reported actually 'seeing' different material. The determinant of their perception, it emerges clearly, is the meaning that the students give to their experience, in this case of X-ray pictures. Abercrombie reports, not surprisingly, that the students were profoundly disconcerted by their learning; if such objective material 'exists' only through personal meaning, how much more must our 'schemata' create the sense of other, less exact, areas of experience? It is the burden of Kelly's (1980) 'theory of personal constructs' that such personal meaning is in fact the key determinant of attitude and behaviour, of personality; our perception is constructed to inform us about different areas of meaning – for example, politics or parenthood – and we have a created interpretation of the world at different levels of complexity. The sense of order is therefore a construction that permeates all aspects of our life and experience.

We rely upon these created perceptions in order to cope in all aspects of our lives; they are basic and pervasive. We change them only with difficulty, precisely because we have to be unconscious of them. Those that are relatively discrete – for example, our understanding of the location of the controls on a car – we can revise without too much difficulty; those that are fundamental – for example, seeing ourselves as able breadwinners for the family – may be so integral a part of our self-image that the material and status changes consequent upon unemployment are, literally, quite inconceivable: we cannot take them in, we cannot put our minds around them. It is this perspective which is the value of Marris's (1974) book *Loss and Change*; he demonstrates the way in which, in nominally quite different spheres, we rely upon such established perception. Our ability to cope is a function of our ability to adapt perception. Bereavement is the most familiar example of such change; there is a similarity in the stages that bereaved people pass through as they try to conceive of the inconceivable, to accept that a loved and (necessarily) taken for granted person is dead. But the process is the same for other change; we may lose locations or roles and, to the extent that they are a fundamental part of our world view, the loss is a loss to that necessary meaning, that 'assumptive world', which has enabled us to cope with our daily lives.

Our coping capacity is thus, in part, always a function of the meaning which we give to our experience; our ability to cope cannot be understood without that meaning. We make a selection – necessarily rich and diverse – from the potentially infinite stimuli we encounter and we impart to it a necessary synthesis; we create our own sense of order. But this creation of meaning is evidently not just a personal process. It is clear that some meanings have a cultural or group homogeneity which suggests that they can, they must, be shared with others – for otherwise family or social life would not be possible. Reality is thus in significant ways also a 'social construction' (Berger and Luckmann, 1967); we learn with and from others the character of particular meanings. Its maintenance is also a social process; particularly in areas where the 'truth' is not easily verified – for example, in political or moral matters – we are conscious of seeking out the company of those who share our views, which relieves us of the (impossible) task of constantly reviewing or revising our beliefs. We thus maintain our necessary sense of order by an essential and entirely routine process of social 'confirmation'. Indeed, the social truth must be kept under surveillance because, in some respect, it *is* constantly revised. The social truth is never absolute; it is negotiated and shifting, and thus always open to change and re-negotiation. We therefore check it carefully and constantly, even in trivial matters. We are unaware of such checking when we say good morning or ask for a fare, but we are quickly alerted if the appropriate reply is not given. Thus the social process of 'confirming' meaning is as fundamental as the psychological process of relying upon meaning; indeed it facilitates that reliance and is therefore a pre-condition of it. Meaning is maintained only by a constant process in which it is understood and shared by other people.

Coping is therefore a function of both the creation and the confirmation of meaning, and these two processes take their place in an understanding of the basis of social work. Social workers are always concerned not with problems *per se*, but with people's capacity to cope with problems. Social work is a personal service. It is this emphasis upon the capacity of the individual (though not necessarily as an individual in isolation) that distinguishes social work. It demands that one element in the social worker's inquiry *always* be the meaning that people give to their experience, because this human meaning is *always* a significant element in the capacity to cope. This emphasis upon meaning is a characteristic of all social work, whether its focus is upon activity, counselling, material aid or planning. 'Meaning', however, is shown to be not only a necessary element in human experience, but a creation of human experience; a creation, moreover, which is maintained only by a process of social communication and exchange. This rather unfamiliar and philosophical ground seems to be the arena for the practice of social work; the common, constant element in social work seems to be a focus upon the understanding and communication of meaning.

THE UNSEEN CHARACTER OF SOCIAL WORK

Social workers do not usually construct their understanding of social work in terms of coping and, in particular, meaning, but they are very familiar with works which in fact rest upon such assumptions; for example, the accounts of mental illness given by R. D. Laing, in which madness is a consequence of the 'disconfirmation' of meaning, and with the accounts of the therapy of Carl Rogers in which the confirmation of meaning (the communication of empathic understanding) is itself and by itself a major therapeutic influence. They thus know that, to a greater or lesser extent, we all need to share our mental and emotional world with other people, that by so doing we maintain or rediscover well-being, and that by failing to do so we fail to cope. But they do not appear to have grasped that this is the basis, the essence, of helping in social work, for it is this interpretation which makes clear the designation '*social* worker'. Individual coping and social well-being rests upon a social process, the successful sharing of unique individual 'meanings'. This is an essential process and it requires that everyone find recognition and acceptance of the infinitely diverse ways in which they create and communicate their experience. Social workers *alone* give their primary professional attention to such meaning; it is the basis of their practice.

Recognition of 'meaning' as its common base gives access to significant avenues for exploration and explanation in social work. Immediately two characteristics are evident. First, the 'problematic' diversity of social work can be seen to be the source of its potential strength, and not – as is so often alleged – a source of weakness. This diversity extends beyond the different locations, methods and problems with which social work is associated, to the very 'stuff' of social work; social work must be about thoughts and feelings, associations and imaginations, biography and culture, because these are the shaping influences, expressed in 'meaning', upon people's coping capacity, motivation and behaviour. Social work must master professionally that same diversity, that creative selection and synthesis, which all of us master as a condition of our very human existence. Secondly, social work is seen to be an activity which can never be professionally exclusive; not only does its practice rest upon the fundamentally 'human' ability to understand meaning, something which of itself cannot be 'professional' at all, but the use of meaning must underlie the communication of all professions. Indeed its use must also be central to the best practice of some other kindred groups, to politics, journalism, education and the church.

Social work has not been clear about its social character and its roots in meaning, and it has been confused by these issues of heterogeneity and lack of exclusivity. This confusion has had a high cost. Social work has not only failed to consolidate its direct work with clients, but significantly failed to develop its wider potential social role, for its task is not only to help individuals and families with the meaning they give to their own experience, but to foster a more public recognition of the meaning of significant common experiences. The task of the social worker is always to understand the meaning of experience and to communicate that understanding. The exploration of the nature of this task, and of its consequences for the necessary knowledge and skill of the social worker, is the focus of the following chapter.

3

Understanding Others: The Basis of Knowledge and Skill in Social Work

UNDERSTANDING – THE FOUNDATION OF HELPING

All people know from experience the need for 'social confirmation' at times of stress; at these times real understanding is
essential for well-being. At such times we seek out those whom
we believe to be particularly understanding. Sometimes this is
expressed in terms of the importance of the potential helper being
able to 'listen', but in this context 'listening' always means a very
active form of a sometimes passive behaviour. In this context, it
always means 'listen and know what I mean' – and thus someone
who understands. Indeed, for many people in need this in itself
seems to be a sufficient support to enable them to regain their
ability to cope; for others it may not be a sufficient but it is still a
necessary process. It is, for example, common to hear about those
offering 'practical' help that their help is inadequate because 'they
do not understand' – not (though this may also be true) that the
practical help is in itself inappropriate.

'Listening and knowing what I mean' is not an easy task. We
are very careful when seeking someone to fill this role; we are
conscious that amongst those we know some will be able to
understand and that others will not, even though those others
may be valued highly in other ways. Our consciousness at such
times if focused entirely upon those things which are important to
us and the need to have them confirmed by others becomes a
matter of profound urgency. Our problem will be in some way

helped if someone does understand and it will be in some way exacerbated if they do not. The sensation of isolation, of loneliness, plays a big part in this experience, as if in some real way 'a problem shared is a problem halved' – the colloquial description acquires real substance in the light of the need for the social confirmation of meaning. The corollary of this is also true; the failure of an attempt to share brings not a resumption of the status quo, but a confirmation of the weight of the problem – for part of its weight is then that it must be borne alone.

This description gives some indication of the task which is required of the helper. It is as if the helper must make a journey with the client so that, because of his first-hand experience, he will then know the sights and experiences which the traveller must encounter; he will know them in detail: he will know the shapes, the sizes and the colours of the objects encountered, the facts and knowledge learned, the emotions felt. The worker will also know the significance of the experience of the journey, what it feels like to be in the midst of these events, places and sensations, not for any traveller, but for this traveller. He will know their particular meanings: associations, memories and evocations. For it is all these things together which constitute the experience of the client traveller, and thus all these things together which the worker traveller must therefore seek to know.

The terms of this description are not a whimsical fantasy. It is part of the problematic nature of social work knowledge that we must somehow characterize the meaning and experience of clients, and find the ways in which the worker will communicate this meaning and experience. This is essential to the job – the worker may know that the family can manage only with the greatest difficulty, but only if he can show the family that he knows something of their experience will he be able to help deal with the stresses and problems they encounter. For unless the family *knows* that someone understands, it cannot diminish the weight of the problem and the space and hope necessary to achieve change is not created. People cannot work for change, and cannot believe that change is possible, unless they can see their experience 'shared' by others, without those others becoming disabled or incapacitated. The worker must know his client's problem almost as if he were living it, and *show* his knowledge, even though it is also a condition of his help that he is in fact

himself simultaneously a coping person. Such exact and pheno-
menologically pervasive knowledge is the basis of trust and
effective helping.

This 'understanding' is then a distinct and subtle matter; it has
to be exact, detailed – a precise recreation of the experiential
world in which the other person finds himself, containing sufficient thought, attitude and feeling, pattern and complexity to be a
rich creation, detailed, complicated and coherent. We know from
our own experience that this is a necessary attribute of the helping
person; we also know from our own experience that such people
are rare – that we note and value them when we find them, and
that we seek them out in particular at times of need because they
are then uniquely able to help. But people do not ordinarily think
of these abilities as being something that can be formally
described, measured or taught because they appear to be abilities
which are personal and unique. Any act of understanding is
peculiar to the people involved, and the ability to understand is
very much part of personality and experience. Yet it is these
abilities which lie at the centre of social work.

The role of understanding is most clearly evident in those
models of social work which emphasize casework or counselling.
It is particularly clear in the work of the 'client-centred therapy'
school, which is increasingly seen to have a special relevance for
social workers (for example, see Egan, 1975, Rogers, 1969,
Truax and Carkhuff, 1967). These theorists hold that a principal
activity of the helper must be some form of 'accurate empathy',
for it is only through such experience that the client will be the
better able to cope with the world. It is experiencing the empathic
helper which is itself the principal therapy. This explains why
many people find it unnecessary to have further help; they find
significant help just in putting to the helper the problem and
through that articulation and understanding they come to a
solution not previously available to them. This is a perspective
which has been extensively researched, and it is clear that the
effectiveness of the helper is very much a quality of the *person* of
the helper, and that some people do help and others impede. The
effective helper must show himself competent in a number of
ways, but the principal one is always that the helper must offer
the client accurate empathic understanding.

The value of this client-centred perspective and its derivatives extends validly to all manner of social work 'interviews' beyond those with clients. Social workers are also substantially engaged in work with those who have other responsibilites for clients or with those who may themselves have the *de facto* responsibility for the social care of clients. Social workers have not always been quick to see that these contacts – indeed any social contacts – must also be characterized by the criteria of understanding, for the worker's object, as helper, will always be to understand a person's perspective and when necessary to help increase its relevant range and utility. This is true as much for the headmaster of the delinquent's school as for the delinquent; it is also true for negotiations within the worker's own agency or any other 'purposeful' encounter. It has been a curious and profoundly misleading belief amongst many social workers that 'professional' skills are only for clients. Such a belief is not only blatantly wrong, because such skills are evidently the articulated skills of social life, but profoundly disrespectful to clients, suggesting that they somehow merit a different attention from 'ordinary people'. Social workers are bound at times to 'social work' their colleagues, their students, and their own friends and families, and it has been an unreal inhibition to suggest they should not do so.

No professional social work contacts require 'only' (it is in fact difficult to master the discipline of such reflective exchange) understanding, but such understanding remains the essential basis of the social worker's practice in all other ways. Just within the 'client-centred model', for example, the worker must decide when it is appropriate to confront the client with his perception of behaviour which does not seem to square with the client's own self-reports, or when to offer the client information about the worker's own feelings or his own life experience. These decisions may be crucial aspects of their interaction; they are not matters that can be left to casual whim. Such interventions have to be as appropriate as the worker's other communications; to be intelligible they too must fit closely the way the client sees and experiences the world. Such decisions are therefore based upon a knowledge of the meaning the client gives to his experience, including his immediate experience of the worker (this knowledge informs what has sometimes been described as the importance of 'timing'). All aspects of counselling interviews, not just listening but also the worker's interventions, are a direct and exact function of the worker's understanding.

Social work includes counselling but, even with individuals, usually exceeds counselling. The term 'casework' has not found favour recently, but the model of 'task-centred casework' proposed by Reid and Epstein (1972) has made it very much easier for social workers to establish simple, intelligible goals and stages in their more active work. The model emphasizes the problem-solving character of casework, and requires that help is concrete, specific and focused. It offers steps and procedures that require the worker to stay close to the client's motivation and meaning, and avoids the destructive complexity and confusion which has characterized some other models of social work. The model is a considerable gain for social work. But the model, no less than a client-centred model, in fact rests upon an exact understanding of the client's meaning, in order to identify, negotiate and establish appropriate objectives and to work in trust towards their realization. The model is based largely implicitly upon an understanding which in the client-centred perspective is largely explicit; indeed the two models are not in contradiction but can be seen as stages of a helping process (as indeed some authors present them) – but as a process which thus assumes a constant exactness of understanding which must be the basis of all the worker's effort.

Understanding as the basis of helping is the basis of social work whatever its form; its role is evident in all other settings in which social workers engage in direct work with clients. Whether the worker largely shares active pastimes with the client or whether he tries to encourage the acquisition of social, bureaucratic, or even political skills, the social worker is a social worker in as much as he tries to enhance coping capacity, and he does this by means of his understanding of the experience of others. This same process constitutes the only plausible basis for a social work role in 'social care planning' as envisaged in the Barclay Report (NISW, 1982); such planning for 'general' groups of clients is social work in as much as it is extrapolation from understanding known experience. But the root knowledge and skill of the social worker is always his understanding of individual human experience, even if it is the understanding of many individuals; its character precludes social work ever being a matter of abstract assertion.

One obvious benefit of the 'generic movement' in social work has been the development of approaches to social work which are evidently more plausible and realistic than their predecessors; the writing of recent years offers workers ways to organize and clarify their practice which seem to be much more directly linked to the experience of practice. For the most part this material is in the form of 'models' – client centred, task centred, unitary 'theory'; social workers can now be very much clearer about the relationship of different elements within their work, elements which were always present but somehow previously critically unseen or confused. Even if some of this new material has a certain jargon, it is not 'mysterious' and its development has contributed enormously to the potential clarification of the nature of social work. But it is significant that these contributions are for the most part models, not theories; they establish relationships and procedures but they still leave to be explained what 'happens' in social work. Indeed, their greater clarity shows up their omissions, for they are all rooted upon an assumed understanding which is not itself a part of the models. These accounts point to the importance of understanding meaning, but they do not help establish the nature of that understanding. So recent contributions towards a practice theory for social work are significant but limited gains. In fact they stick at exactly that same point which has always frustrated attempts to give a proper account of social work.

THE CHARACTERISTICS OF UNDERSTANDING IN SOCIAL WORK

This understanding of the social worker is a subtle and complex creation; its elements are rich and varied – facts and feelings, experiences, associations and attitudes, the infinite variety of elements that constitute our mental life. It is also, of necessity, a unique creation; it is not only a blend of great diversity but is created always on and for one occasion, for it must be always exact in circumstances which are always distinct. The social worker's understanding is therefore an elusive creation, but it is not a mysterious creation, for it is also that same process of understanding which any person uses to understand another.

Such understanding may elude precise description, but it does not preclude all description or access; for example, as human beings, we believe that to say that one person can understand another, and that he can do so for better or for worse, has meaning. Such description may be common sense, but it is also obviously the fundamental sense of the social worker. Social work therefore has no choice but to explore and recognize this sense and to use any or all perspectives which can offer good access to it. The first step in such exploration is to identify the perceptible characteristics of such understanding.

The worker's first task is to establish his own evaluation of the client's meaning; it is this 'meaning' given by the client to his experience which shapes the nature of the problem and of the response of the worker. It is the most important characteristic of the worker's understanding that he can only make sense of this meaning because he knows about it from his own experience. This is not to assert that the worker must have himself undergone the problem faced by the client. Such specific experiences may be helpful, but only if it is the experience of someone who is generally understanding; specific experience is not of itself any qualification. The important requirement is that the worker understands the general nature of the experience of his client.

The worker knows about the client's meaning because the worker's own 'human nature' tells him what it is to experience, for example, intellectual confusion or particular emotional intensity, even though his own experience is in other specific circumstances; he only knows the character of his client's meaning because he himself knows, in general, what it is to experience such mental or emotional states and can sensitively extrapolate from them. The worker understands to the extent that he is sensitively familiar with his own experience, but not because of the specific nature or intensity of that experience. He understands confusion not because he has experienced *this* confusion but because he has been confused; he understands loss, depression or love because of his own experience of loss, depression or love. This is a necessary condition of all human understanding; we understand others not by detached scrutiny (although this has a place), but by this essential and spontaneous reference to experience; it is a reference to our own common human nature. We learn the detail, the specific circumstances, of the experience of others by their exposition, but we know its fundamental character only because we can ourselves give it meaning. This process is most familiar to social workers through the concept of loss; Marris's (1974) description of the common character of loss means that everyone must have within them, through some loss experience, the seeds of an understanding of other such experiences. So, for example, an experience of bereavement may be the basis of an understanding of divorce or unemployment. The worker need not have experienced the client's particular circumstances, but it is nonetheless the meaning of the worker's own experience which enables him to be understanding. The principal characteristic of the worker's understanding is therefore that it must ncessarily be a function of the meaning which he gives, spontaneously or intuitively, to his own experience.

An emphasis upon the worker's own intuitive ability to 'make meaning' is also essential in other ways; his status as a participant in a significantly social (albeit professional) situation inevitably places demands upon his own perceptual ability. The worker is faced with a vast range of material which could claim his attention, some of it about the client's experience, some about his own, some of it descriptive data about the client's circumstances and biography, some of it general knowledge about the type of problems that the client faces, some of it knowledge about available resources and opportunity, and so on. The material hugely exceeds the limits of any manageable whole and so must be the subject of some selection to make a viable synthesis. The worker's professional competence rests upon the quality of this selection and synthesis, upon his ability to create an adequate 'picture' of the circumstances and situation. The worker's choice will be guided – to an extent – by his formal learning of relevant knowledge, ideology and philosophy, but the specific process will be one which is intuitive; in Abercrombie's and Kelly's terms (see above, Chapter 2), it can only be guided by his 'schemata' and his 'constructs'. These *may* reflect this learning but his perception is likely to be as much influenced by his previous colloquial learning as by his professional education, for it is a notorious educational problem to translate the insights of generalized teaching into specific situations. The need to achieve this translation, as will be seen, must come to make distinct demands upon social work education.

This emphasis upon the worker's capacity to create his own picture of the client's world – his creativity – is necessarily an emphasis upon intuition, for the process of 'making order' is not only a necessary but a necessarily spontaneous process. We may sometimes review and revise our creation, and we may sometimes attempt deliberately to alter our general guiding constructs, but the process of selection and synthesis is an immediate and an intuitive process, and cannot be otherwise. The worker's reliance upon this intuition is increased by his lack of opportunity for subjecting his perception to such review and revision; it is in the nature of social work that important judgements about helping practice are immediate judgements, and thus the worker is necessarily committing himself in action to decisions derived from his immediate consciousness. This is most evident in the worker's communication of his understanding of the meaning that others give to their experience. This understanding, as has been noted, must be shared or it is useless, and so either explicitly, or incidentally in the course of other activity, the worker must be able to tell the client of this understanding. This communication has, in part at least, to be *immediate*, for the need arises in the course of conversation and the worker is shown to be understanding (or not) by the quality of his next reply to the client. I help according to the way I 'am' now, not the way I will reply next week; a client who is distressed or angry requires some immediate response, not to reply tomorrow or in five minutes (a matter not to be confused with the reply to practical inquiries which, despite the common anxieties of beginning workers, can nearly always await research). The worker must thus draw his communication directly from his consciousness, and so it is inevitably an expression of intuitive meaning.

The intuitive character of this communication is also evident in its articulation. The worker has to be able to get across his sense of a creation which is rich, subtle and varied, and he has to do so in a way which will make sense in everyday terms. His language will have to be expressive, personal, evocative and concrete. He will have to be not only fluent but immediately, spontaneously fluent, quick and clear at putting his meaning into words. His communications must also be conveyed in other ways; his behaviour must at all times be consistent with his understanding, for his behaviour is witness to the genuineness of his meaning. His behaviour is also sometimes the necessary vehicle for his understanding, for many people express and perceive meaning and understanding primarily in action, symbolically rather than explicitly. 'Doing things' with and for clients is not a substitute for understanding but an expression of it, and the understanding must be no less exact because it is not explicitly articulated. The worker has to 'live' his understanding; to fail to do so is not only hypocrisy and bad faith, but the frustration of his helping aspirations. In these matters the worker has no choice, for understanding is never concealed in any middle ground; words and behaviour suggest either understanding or its absence.

There is one other, more generally recognized way in which the social worker's understanding draws upon his immediate consciousness. To help his clients he must be able to make ready and imaginative use of his personal experience with his clients and his experience of them. He must be quickly aware of what he notices about the behaviour of the client with himself. He must, for example, be quickly aware of the ways in which that behaviour seems to 'fit' with the client's reported experience – reported acquiescence may be an ill accompaniment to perceived hostility. The worker must also have quick access to his own immediate emotions; if he feels himself hostile or protective towards his client, then he must know and note this, and be prepared to make use of it at the time. A key element in his 'picture' is his own spontaneous reaction to his client.

Whilst this last element in the worker's 'purposeful use of self' is one which is familiar from the 'psychoanalytic tradition' of casework, it is now evident that the 'use of self' is a much more fundamental matter for social work; it in fact defines both the social worker's practice knowledge and his practice behaviour. This initial exploration has suggested that the worker's understanding includes a necessarily intuitive grasp of the client's meaning, that the worker necessarily relies upon his intuitive perception, and that the necessary immediate and fluent expression of this perception is an intuitive process. This understanding is an integral part of the worker's self and thus the worker gains his understanding, in part at least, not by a struggle to explore external issues but by trying to deploy and articulate his own consciousness. So there is something of a play within a play. The worker's primary task is to understand the meaning of his client and to communicate that understanding, but the construction and communication of that understanding are possible only through the worker's own meaning, only through the way in which the worker himself sees the world.

Social workers annoy and mystify their critics because they often explain their professional conduct with such terms as 'it felt right' or 'I just knew that was how they felt'. It can be seen now that their reliance upon these terms, while insufficient, is a necessary matter; it properly describes what happens. Their understanding and action stem intimately from their consciousness, and this 'intuitive use of self' can be seen to be the central process in social work. It determines the nature and use of the social worker's knowledge, which is expressed in his own 'meaning', and it determines his significant skill, which is the articulation of that meaning. It makes it clear that the primary responsibility of the institutions which select, educate and employ social workers is to identify the quality of this personal intuition and to ensure it is maintained and enhanced.

INTUITION IN SOCIAL WORK THEORY AND PRACTICE

An emphasis upon the worker's intuitive knowledge and intuitive behaviour, upon the 'use of self', as the centre of the analysis of social work is not promising ground to those who seek empricial precision. But 'precision', in the sense used by the empiricist researcher, is not a plausible property of meaning and understanding, and it is the inevitable importance of these processes in social work which in turn require an emphasis upon the worker's intuition. It is an emphasis which leads eventually to the possibility, to the necessity, that social work acknowledges a rather different manner of precision, a precision which is entirely exacting, but which belongs to another tradition of knowledge and inquiry. Prior steps are necessary, however, before exploring this alternative perspective. The first is to establish the implications of the use of intuition and the importance of their proper recognition.

Acceptance of this emphasis upon the social worker's 'use of self' immediately gives access to some of the perennial problems in social work theory; it does so not by 'solving' them in the terms of previous inquiry, but by offering scope for their redefinition in a more realistic and a more useful fashion. By so doing social work can come to make some sense of familiar problems – the place it gives to learned knowledge and to specialization, the assertions that social work is a matter of values and attitudes, the integration of knowledge and the integration of theory into practice. Above all, through the possibility of an accessible precision, social work can aspire to a procedure for evaluation, to the possibility of debate about 'good' and 'bad' social work. It is this possibility, of a framework for the evaluation of social work, which makes this discussion an urgent and practical matter, for above all else social work is hampered by the absence of any recognized way of assessing competence. Acceptance of the necessary emphasis upon the worker's intuitive use of self, far from precluding the possibility of evaluation, as some have feared, in fact proves eventually to offer the means whereby social work *can* be assessed.

To identify social work as a process of understanding the meaning that people give to their experience is to emphasize the ordinary character of social work. Social work does become a matter of 'common sense', just as its critics have often alleged – although it will become evident that social workers must have uncommonly good common sense. Social workers 'understand' others in the way that everyone understands the experience of others. The 'meanings' which are the content of this understanding are concrete and diverse, always idiosyncratic, by their very nature never the 'property' of any technical professional. Their place at the centre of social work explains both social work's distinctive concern with individuals and the way in which its consciousness of the individual characterizes its approach to groups and bigger populations: this approach is identified in a quite different – but, it will be seen later, entirely relevant – context by Raymond Williams (1965): 'We attend with our whole senses to every aspect of the general life, yet the centre of value is always in the individual human person – not any one isolated person, but the many persons who are the reality of the general life.'

Social work will therefore never have any genuinely exclusive knowledge, nor its practitioners any exclusive competence; there will always be people who have an unusually developed yet untrained ability to understand others and to act upon that understanding. Social work can only be distinct because of the *reliability* with which its workers master such an unusually developed understanding. Such understanding may be a competence of those in many, and any, other spheres, but for other professions it is not a necessary competence; it may always be desirable but it is often, even usually, lacking. But for social workers it is the only competence which gives their work identity, and for their clients it is only because social workers can offer such exact understanding that their help exceeds the more technical and more specific service of others. The ability of the social worker in any field rests first and foremost upon this competence, and his understanding must consequently be reliably exact and profound.

The role of understanding in social work makes much clearer the problematic character of 'a body of knowledge' for social work. Despite considerable heart searching over the years social work has been unable to agree the areas of knowledge which must be learned to inform its practice. The diversity of its fields of activity and the quantity of specialist knowledge which is associated with each one has offered critics the obvious charge that social work is blatantly unable to master even a fragment of so much information. It is not surprising that social work has been unable to answer this charge, for it is unanswerable. But neither has social work usually challenged the grounds on which the charge is based, or grasped that the premises of the charge are mistaken. For social work has no need to apologize for its failure to acquire knowledge of universal detail, because the social worker's base knowledge is his understanding of others, not the specific detail which may relate to it. The social worker's 'practice knowledge' is his understanding of his clients; it is this unique understanding which informs and determines his helping. Its only general character, and thus the social worker's only truly general learning, is its basis in the general processes of perception and the creation of meaning which determine the individual's capacity to cope.

This description does not dictate that social workers need no other knowledge or that specialization is inappropriate. It does explain the subsidiary and incomplete nature of the social worker's more particular knowledge. The role of the worker's 'defined' knowledge is to inform his understanding: he will understand more or understand quicker because of his professional learning. Thus the worker who is familiar with the theories of loss and change will be more quickly sensitive and responsive to problems of loss and change; similarly, the worker will be more, or more quickly, sensitive to the problems of old, mentally ill or delinquent people if he has rehearsed some of the possible features of their experience. But this is the use of such knowledge – to anticipate experience; and it is useful only in as much as it is incorporated into the worker's general (perhaps 'personal' is a more apt word) knowledge and available to inform his intuitive knowledge and intuitive behaviour. The real test of the worker's learning is never in his ability to show mastery of abstract knowledge, but in the way such knowledge is plundered and fragmented to inform his practice; his formal learning becomes useful in as much as it is inseparable and indistinguishable from his colloquial learning. The worker may at times wish formally to enunciate or substantiate his understanding – for example, to confirm the likely validity of his judgements – but in practice the knowledge is intuition; its clarification is *post hoc*.

This role for knowledge in social work makes clear that there can be no sufficient curriculum for the profession; it is in the nature of the social worker's task that he will encounter diversity greater than that for which he can be specifically prepared, not least because each situation will be specifically distinct. Social workers can be prepared in general terms for situations which they will probably encounter, but they must be clear – and not apologetic – that such knowledge only serves to sketch in the likely dominant characteristics of experience. Their learning, in fact, ought to tell them that their knowledge has a highly selective character, that its utility lies only in its incorporation within their repertoire of available, intuitive schemata, and that their knowledge is always subsidiary to their assessment of each situation. Their knowledge exists to inform their understanding, not to dominate it; abstract knowledge in social work, whilst it remains abstract knowledge, is utterly useless. A pervasive use of self is the crucial centre point of social work, and its recognition, while not displacing formal approaches to the role, requires absolutely that they show their consistency with it.

Social work, it is increasingly evident, *is* a matter of attitude and value, constructs and ideology. This does not render knowledge irrelevant, but makes clear that the role of knowledge is to inform such perception. Social workers ought to take comfort from the increasing awareness that other professionals also operate in somewhat the same way – it is, for example, suggested in some medical circles that doctors often cannot 'know' what is wrong with their patients and that many doctors, particularly general practitioners, find themselves unwillingly trapped in an unreal stereotype of omniscience. Very few people can have genuinely 'hard' knowledge; indeed, if they could have such knowledge their activity could frequently be made mechanical or bureaucratic. Nonetheless, social work is distinct because of the extent of its reliance upon subjective information and its lack of relatively precise knowledge. But the social need for a 'body of knowledge' is an insidiously pressing one; schoolteachers show this most clearly when they emphasize their subject allegiance (when possible) as their professional knowledge, at the cost of the knowledge of learning processes and development which must be at least as important to their role. Groups which can claim a 'subject' area, a visible body of knowledge, feel impelled by social value to do so.

Social work has no subject area in this way, and attempts to marshall it into one – most notably the quasi-legal field of welfare rights – have been unsuccessful because they so clearly remove social work from the area of its greatest utility. Yet social workers have not been clear or confident about this inability to articulate a basis of specific knowledge; it has been clear that they do not make systematic use of their theoretical knowledge (e.g. Carew, 1979), but not why they do not do so. The result is a confusion about the way in which social workers *can* use theory, to inform their learned constructs; the fact that the worker's 'professional knowledge' becomes his 'personal knowledge' does not remove from the worker any obligation to be as informed as possible. Rather, it means that he has to ensure that 'the 'person' becomes informed, that his own understanding is appropriately broad, subtle and complex. Formal learning, if it is real learning, is one of the significant ways of increasing such understanding. But the understanding that is eventually achieved will be selective and subjective because only in this way can the worker develop a diverse picture which looks anything like the diverse world experienced and perceived by the client. Such understanding is inevitably used by others, by everyone, but social workers are particularly charged with its accomplished mastery. If they can become confident about this mastery, their distinctive use of knowledge can become a skill that they can help others learn – not a cause for misplaced regret.

This explanation of the way in which the social worker makes use of knowledge in turn explains the way in which the worker integrates knowledge, or integrates one theoretical perspective with others; it is an aspect of intuition. Social workers must use diverse perspectives to make intelligible situations which are diverse. Phenomena are explained by the imposition upon them of ordered templates which are sufficiently appropriate; the order is not inherent in them but created by perception. The worker gives situations their 'meaning', and his meaning – like any person's – is a result of the application of learned constructs. The social worker, however, has acquired some of his perspectives as the result of 'formal' learning, and is thus apparently posed the problem of accounting for his use of this learning. But the problem is no different from the general problems of perception, because the worker's professional perception *is* 'general perception'; his understanding is a matter of intuitive consciousness, and explanation can only be a subsequent unravelling and evaluation of intuitive selection and synthesis. The worker may be able to articulate his formal learning, but its integration is an intuitive and an ordinary procedure.

This problem also explains the problem of the integration of theory with practice. This is sometimes presented as the need for an explained link between the general and the particular. In fact, social work in this respect is charged with issues which are not of its creation, for these are partly the general problems of assessing the utility of social science theories, which are assumed (incorrectly) to be the rationale for social work practice. Such theory is often abstract, purporting to explain the links between 'ideal-type' elements, but *in practice* such elements are neither abstract nor ideal. The 'translation' of the theory therefore inevitably poses problems, particularly because the theories are rarely devised as prescriptions for practice. In fact, of course, they are not prescriptions; they inform the worker's understanding and thus his action, but they do not constitute that understanding.

It is not the case, it must be emphasized, that social workers use no theory; all people use theory as the basis of their 'assumptive world' (although they may not see it as theory) and the theory informs their 'schemata', or their way of seeing things. The social worker's perception will be distinct partly because it has been informed explicitly by that formal learning which he has found sufficiently plausible and coherent to incorporate within his existing 'world view', partly because the social worker must be quicker at checking and correcting his intuitive understanding. The worker's 'emotional distance', so often commended, is in fact partly to enable him to move from the general to the particular and back, in a constant shuttle, to see if 'things feel right'. His perceptions can be likened to a series of constant approximations, in which he attempts to relate general and abstract propositions to specific people and situations – not necessarily a conscious process but a necessary one. The theory cannot 'fit', because it is general; the worker's use is necessarily partial and selective; the situation changes with each moment and movement in the client's world. Thus the screening of available understandings is a constant process, fuelled by the worker's need to 'make sense', and revised and reasserted whenever sense is absent. It is an intuitive process. It is extended and articulated by the worker's familiarity with theory, but the appropriate use of theory and its integration into understanding and action is a matter of the accuracy of the worker's intuition.

The help of the social worker, therefore, is not in significant ways distinct from the help that people receive informally. We all experience the support of sharing and understanding in our lives; the social worker offers such help to people who are not getting sufficient support, either because of their isolation or because of the intensity or nature of their needs. His help is different in detail or degree, but not in kind. But it is different in its formality – a formality determined not by any style of dress or address (the use of jeans or Christian names), but because it is offered formally. The worker, unlike friend or family, is required to be purposeful and personally disinterested, because this purpose is the only justification for his involvement. In other words, helping in social work is not a different kind of activity, but the worker has to do deliberately and with maximum effect what others may do spontaneously and without responsibility. It is in this proposition that the idiosyncratic character of social work is most clearly revealed; to do social work is to do purposefully and deliberately that which is primarily intuitive.

To assert that social work makes significant 'use of self' is not a new assertion. It is not normally clear, however, that this use of self extends far beyond the worker's emotional involvement and in fact determines the character of his professional knowledge and behaviour. Competence in social work therefore will be found not by seeking to avoid intuition, but by its recognition and development, by the creation of uncommon common sense. Social work is a matter of intuitive understanding, but it must be intuition which is unusually sound, unusually fluent and accessible, and subject to unusually careful evaluation. The absence of a framework for such evaluation in social work is the biggest single expression of the confusion about social work's character, and also one of the biggest obstacles to social work's wider plausibility. Social work can achieve no effective evaluation if it denies its essentially intuitive character. This character does in fact (it will be shown later) offer social work some means of appreciation and evaluation, those means associated with familiar traditions and procedures which recognize the holistic nature of human experience. There is no way though in which the place of intuitive understanding in social work can be ignored or underplayed. Yet this is not the way in which social work seems usually to have been approached.

4

The Persistent Mystery
of the
Intuitive Use of Self

A STUBBORN AMBIGUITY IN PRACTICE

The concept of the 'use of self' has a long-established place in social work thinking. It has, curiously, both a central and a marginal place. It is central because accounts of social work have consistently recognized the importance of the worker's behaviour and relationship with the client, especially in accounts of social casework. It is marginal because, despite this recognition, the process has been one generally seen as inaccessible to analysis or proper discussion. So it is conspicuous but neither explored nor understood. In effect social work is little better off than the many other groups which assume that the *application* of knowledge is a self-evident matter, either too simple to teach or inherently unteachable. It is already clear though that in social work it is not possible to make a division between the actor and his knowledge – that the knowledge is realized only by the worker. So for the social worker the nature of this 'use of self' is an issue too central, too essential, to be given only a marginal theoretical status; it is a problem which must be solved.

The ambiguity surrounding this 'use of self' is immediately discernible in the everyday experience and institutions of social work. Although it is not usually described in the terms 'intuitive knowledge' and 'intuitive behaviour', it is certainly a common-place amongst social workers that social work puts real and considerable personal demands upon its practitioners. Indeed, for many people this is one of its principle attractions; they seek a job which is more 'real' than others, one in which they feel they 'can be themselves'. Such descriptions focus upon issues of personal engagement, emotion and value: social work is distinct because its workers are necessarily themselves wholly involved and because their professional focus is upon the shifting and varied complexity of people's 'whole' lives, not upon narrowly defined and functional matters. Colloquial descriptions of social work place a considerable emphasis upon the experience of the worker, his own feeling and perception; indeed, good descriptions of social work usually include a very distinct evocative or imaginative element which helps establish the worker's subjective view of the situation. Formal accounts of social workers' perceptions are not easy to come by, but Prins's (1974) article about the motivation of social workers points to an emphasis upon the use of self as an important factor.

The institutions of social work reflect this emphasis upon the personality and attitude of the worker. It is perhaps most evident in the practice of 'supervision'. By tradition, supervision (regular supportive meetings between the worker and a nominated supervisor) constitutes a source of personal support for the worker, a somewhat uncertain recognition that his own perception and behaviour lie at the centre of his work. It has been characterized particularly as confirmation of the worker's *emotional* involvement – that he can work only at personal cost to himself and that some personal support is therefore necessary to sustain this commitment. The role of supervision has often been questioned, but it has up to now been generally maintained, despite significant costs in time and resources to agency and worker. Thus, both agency and worker appear to have had a high investment in this recognition of the worker's personal involvement. The rationale has not, perhaps, been articulate, but it has evidently been important.

A similar focus upon 'personal development' is common in social work education, by tradition through a focus upon 'personal tutorials'. This emphasis was associated with social work's one-time (professed) theoretical basis in psychoanalytic-style models of helping. This link between tutorials and a psychoanalytic orientation is not in any way a necessary one, but where the diminishing emphasis upon this orientation has led to a decline in the use of tutorials, other ways of focusing upon personal development have often gained currency, for example the use of group procedures for sensitivity training. Most educational institutions also place a considerable emphasis upon personal suitability and aptitude in selection for training. Thus the 'use of self', in some way, is a significant theme in much of the education of social workers.

But if there are grounds for thinking that intuitive knowledge and behaviour are a persistent presence in social work, there are also grounds for concluding that their role is not clear, and that their value is disputed. It would not, for example, be a criterion for appointment to a social work role that the applicant should be a master of evocative and imaginative description. Agency records encourage an emphasis upon procedure and formality, and agency organization increasingly reflects an impersonal perspective. Indeed, social workers are frequently accused of intellectual woolliness because of their lack of objectivity and, although the charge is often justified, social workers seem to be no better than their critics in distinguishing between necessary (and perhaps very precise) subjectivity and intellectual vagueness or confusion. So social work is in fact often under attack because of its intuitive character, and social workers collude with this criticism by their silence or apology.

As a result the institutional recognition of intuition is by no means secure; its presence seems somehow inevitable but unwelcome, and in some quarters under explicit assault. Some courses do not include an explicit emphasis upon self-awareness, self-development and personal skills; indeed, there have been suggestions that even personal interviews are an unnecessary process for selection into social work education, despite the fact that such training always involves substantial responsibility for agency work with clients. In some agencies supervision is not routinely available or encouraged; indeed supervision is seen as an increasingly ambiguous process and approached with increasing suspicion. Its purpose is challenged, partly because its practice and rationale have been difficult to articulate, and partly because, perhaps as a result of that difficulty, it has often, quite inappropriately, become no more than the vehicle for the bureaucratic surveillance of social workers. Indeed it is a puzzle to non-social workers that social work should, in any form, need such a costly 'person based' system of support, and social workers have not been able to establish a readily intelligible case to explain this need; at times of economic stress such inability places these resources at evident risk.

The intuitive use of self in social work seems neither to go away nor to become clear; like those grand social work objectives – with which it is evidently and inextricably linked – it haunts the institutions of social work as an embarrassment or a puzzle rather than the necessary source of creative professional energy. It is an inevitable presence, but social workers do not know how to deal with it. Its development is too often half-hearted or reluctant, yet for some unseen reason it seems difficult to abandon. Not surprisingly, this is reflected in its treatment in the social work literature.

INTUITION – NOTED BUT UNEXPLORED

The approach to the 'worker's use of self' in social work literature is by no means always 'half-hearted'; it is its treatment which has lacked a sufficiently developed discussion. It is certainly not difficult to establish that social work has traditionally recognized the importance of such intuition; references are scattered throughout the literature, ranging from those which give it an instrumental place to those in which it is necessary but somehow incidental. The problem of these uses of intuition is not any inherent lack of validity (although some older material is given an emphasis which today can seem precious and pretentious), but the lack of any discussion about the philosophical or practical implications of the use of such intuition. The references are not wrong, but insufficient.

Discussion of intuition does not usually make use of such a specific term; it appears in different guises. The most prominent of these, and the one which has also attracted the most scepticism, is the 'use of relationship'. This was a particularly important emphasis in those models of social casework which leant upon psychoanalytic theory as their intellectual basis. Within these models the worker must attend carefully to the way in which he and the client relate, and the feelings and responses they arouse in each other. These feelings and responses will be an essential part of 'treatment'; they will both yield information which might otherwise be inaccessible ('this must be how he treats his father'), and they offer a unique medium for communication – the client learns through the experience of an emotionally significant relationship. Much of the client's learning, within such a model, is deemed to be either unconscious, or only conscious because of the insights which the worker has helped him acquire; the worker must look also to the importance of his own unconscious.

The suspicion which such an account now often arouses is justified because of the mystery associated with this emphasis upon the unconscious; social work should not mystify, for its value lies not in the obscurity but in the quality of the worker's understanding. But a rejection of the emphasis upon a pseudo-psychoanalytic approach has been something of a 'baby and the bathwater' problem, for social work evidently continues to rely upon a 'use of self' which was relatively well-established within such a framework. The work of the proponents of such an approach (for example, Biestek, 1957; Ferard and Hunnybun, 1962; Hollis, 1964) has little contemporary currency, yet it remains no less important that clients and workers learn through their experience of genuinely significant relationships.

Lydia Rapoport was a social work writer whose work, it will be seen later, is particularly interesting because it did point to some of the implications of the purposeful use of self. The following passage serves to illustrate some of the qualities often associated with 'the relationship'.

> The helping relationship is the central dynamic in the helping activity. The social worker is the direct instrument of professional help. His focus must therefore be on the helping relationship: its meaning, its vagaries, its potential for further growth and self direction. Purposeful use of relationships calls for a high capacity in the social worker for the tolerance and absorption of all kinds of negative feelings, massive anxieties and needs by clients and groups; it calls for a high degree of self awareness and self control. In order to master the controlled, conscious and imaginative use of self, the social work practitioner must possess a high degree of maturity, and a deep sense of personal and social responsibility. (Rapoport, 1960)

Rapoport here avoids the most mysterious possibilities of such description, but she makes very clear the considerable, and necessary, emphasis upon the person of the worker. Her description is still a useful one for social work. But the utility of such descriptions in general has been challenged because of their apparent subjectivity and inaccessibility. Such descriptions do not lend themselves to precise analysis, nor lead to easily evaluated practice – the qualities which social work has come to believe it must seek. For this reason social work has not known how to receive or make use of such descriptions, and without exploration of the implications of such emphasis (which even Rapoport failed adequately to conduct) their value is ignored because they are not seen to be relevant.

An emphasis upon the relationship lurks within the more contemporary literature with the same stubborn tenacity that is evident in practice. Priestley *et al.* (1978) offer an example of the way in which the issue is slowly, almost begrudgingly, but inevitably recognized. They write with a robust and effective determination to maintain simplicity; they note that counselling may be indispensable to many forms of personal change, and necessary to acquire skills, but warn against the danger of irrelevant emotional complexity, against helping styles in which 'the ends of the endeavour are less than clear to both participants, and the means of achieving them sometimes obscured by jargon and bureaucratic procedure'. It is, they note, 'curious to observe the song and dance that is made about the art of interviewing by some of those who make a living out of it'. Their cautions are entirely necessary; common sense has often been forsaken in descriptions of helping. But it must be noted that their cautions are a preliminary to their recognition of the subtlety and subjectivity of the helping process, a warning word as they lead the reader, as they must, on to the uncertain ground that indicates the value of relationship, trust and empathy to the importance of becoming skilled in interviewing (and how little attention is ordinarily devoted to it). They observe that 'the shape and content of the helping encounter pass quickly beyond all possible hope of reconstruction ... partly due to the elusive nature of much human interaction'.

Other writers, writing from very different standpoints, have had very obvious doubts about social work's perceived preoccupation with matters of personal change and the consequent use of relationships. They have conceded that such issues must remain an element within social work, but their argument has been about its emphasis. Cohen (1975) argues that no 'radical social work' can disregard the importance of personal helping. Jehu (1967), exploring the importance of 'learning theory in social work', notes that while others have given a rather different role to the use of relationship, even within his own perspective it may be 'corrective' and its important components will include 'warmth, sympathy, attention, interest, concern and professional discretion and competence' – qualities which he does not explore, but which evidently rely heavily upon the worker's use of self.

A report of an American symposium (Clark, Arkava and Associates, 1979) is particularly interesting in this context. It shows the persistence of an emphasis upon the use of self in very different theoretical contexts and at times when social work is under pressure to give very specific evidence of precision and purpose. The symposium was convened to identify the 'competences' which make for effective social work; it was emphasized that in a hostile economic climate it was necessary to show those who control the budget and look for productivity just what social workers do and how they do it. Yet there appears in the symposium the familiar vast objectives for social work, and the persistent emphasis upon relationship and the use of self. 'The essential capacity of social workers', note Zastrow and Navarre (1979), '. . . is the ability to counsel and relate to people'; they cite general support from the literature for this criterion. Wiegand (1979) asserts that 'the capabilities of a helping person appear to be as much the product of life experience as they are of professional education'; he goes on to note that 'competence is the capacity of a person to engage his full range of abilities appropriately'. Indeed, to Wiegand, the social worker is like the sculptor who 'frees the sculpted form from the marble', in that the worker recognizes the potential of the client and enables him to achieve that potential. 'It is quite obvious', reports Wiegand, 'that [these social work processes] are the work of an artist as well as a scientist.' This description, it will be seen later, belongs in a significant line of undeveloped analogies between social work and art; but its present importance is the evocative emphasis upon subjectivity despite the need to determine, with precision, the aims and procedures of competent social work.

This quality of reflection under duress might also be seen to characterize the deliberations of the Barclay Report (NISW, 1982), which many thought was initiated by the government to examine social work at a time of great suspicion about its practice. The working party explicitly – and correctly – does not list the 'role and tasks' of social workers, which had been the focus of its terms of reference; it notes that social workers must be called upon to fill many roles and undertake many diverse tasks, and thus that social work cannot be identified by these features. It notes approvingly evidence that social workers must acquire a 'synthesis of knowledge which approaches ... closely the totality of the client in his situation'; it asserts that social workers should always show a 'respect for persons and ... see other people in all the complexity of their life, relationships and environment'; and it points out that social workers need particularly to understand their own personalities, prejudices and attitudes. In these, and in many other ways, the working party recognizes the intuitive character which is the essential and central core of social work, yet it does so in the context of an inquiry in which specificity and clarity about social work were the explicit purpose.

This report from the Barclay Committee repeats, typically, the approach of many other social work studies which note, implicitly or explicitly, the idiosyncratic character of social work but fail adequately to give it explanation or analysis. The Committee refers to the intuitive, subjective character of social work, but does not explain the nature or implications of such a character. The result of such omission in the past has been a failure, by social workers as well as others, adequately to understand this basic character and thus to misconstruct the organizations and institutions which govern social work. It seems likely that this latest attempt at clarification, whatever organizational changes result from it, will fail for the same reasons: it notes but does not properly identify the fundamentally distinctive character of social work.

The social worker's use of self, of intuition, has been consistently recognized as a distinct aspect of helping in social work. It is sometimes given significant emphasis and described in detail. But the terms 'recognition' and 'description' are appropriate ones; this process is not usually the subject of development or analysis – its assertion poses problems but these problems are not explored. There is, it seems, at the centre of social work a difficult area that deters or even precludes analysis; it is noted, sometimes with enthusiasm, sometimes uneasily, and left.

OBJECTIONS TO INTUITION

An understanding of intuition can, it is already clear, offer social work a way towards a 'practice theory', towards an exploration of its means of integrating theory with practice and theory with theory. There has in fact been some recognition of the way in which intuitive knowledge and intuitive behaviour are connected with these problems of integration; the issue of intuition is not *always* just noted and left. But recognition characteristically sees intuition not as something given and essential, but as an obstacle or problem to be removed, as a matter to be deplored. The emphasis in such an approach is not upon the inevitability of intuition and the need for reliable and sound intuition, but upon the importance of obviating or minimizing its use. Writers look to the fuller development of a 'scientific' approach, either implicitly seeking to avoid the intuitive use of self, or explicitly challenging its role – but failing in fact to make the challenge complete.

Solomon (1976) is typical of social work writers who have noted the difficulties of linking social work theory with practice. He writes:

> The development of effective practice theory depends on the effective translation of behavioural science theory into an action system for problem solving ... the bridging concepts and principles have been far too few and much too vague. What is required ... is a more effective methodology or methodologies for connecting behavioural science theory with theories of practice.

Solomon is arguing that social work has allowed behavioural science theories which explain phenomena to co-exist with intervention models (which he also calls practice theories) which structure professional behaviour, but that social work has not been able to make any articulate link between the two. He notes, correctly, the advantage of the recent development of models of intervention which are not rooted in theories of behaviour. But he goes on to search for a scientific bridge between them: 'what is needed is a more effective technique for the integration of general theories of human behaviour with specific theories of practice'. Solomon, like others, sees an unsolved problem, but, like others, his search for a solution is directed into areas that *cannot* yield a sufficient answer.

Emanuel Tropp (1976), contributing to the same collection of essays, is more robust and aggressive in his approach to this problem: 'We must ask ourselves why we have so much trouble agreeing on the mere description of our own landscape even though, when faced with the most far fetched, not clearly defined ideas from non-social work sources, we buy them unhesitatingly.' It is, not surprisingly, to the sciences that Tropp turns for his 'solution'; he makes comparison with the physical sciences, in particular the chemist's analysis of elements: he says that social workers 'have hardly begun to define their 'elements' ... If we can specify what the components of a single knowledge cell are, we are then in a position to begin to connect those components.' Tropp's article offers a particularly good illustration of the nature of the problem. It is not that Tropp is wrong to assume a difficulty with social work theory; it is not even that his enthusiastic commitment to a rational, positivistic approach is unhelpful, for such an attitude (up to a point) would clearly benefit social work. It is that Tropp's approach is blatantly incomplete. Tropp in fact states that social work cannot be a certain science, but nonetheless only advocates the pursuit of greater certainty. He ignores the immediate implication of his recognition of uncertainty, which is that if uncertainty and subjectivity are necessary features of social work, one necessary task is to identify how it must be managed; if intuition is a fact it is evidently insufficient merely to note but then to ignore it. Indeed Tropp not only ignores this uncertainty; he mocks it. He then only looks for 'more science' when he knows that science cannot be sufficient. This is a typical response to the dilemma, and so the gap between theory and practice, and between theory and theory, has remained.

But to plead for more science is not the only response to the dilemma. Howe (1980) notes many of the necessary features of social work, in particular its grand goals and the infinite elasticity of its relevant knowledge. He shows, plausibily, that social work cannot possibly be a 'scientific' activity if it cannot be more precisely defined or measured; and he uses the rather appropriate term 'baroque' to describe the plethora of theory which social workers are asked nominally to master. But Howe, unlike the soldiers of science who advocate 'pushing on', seems to advocate 'withdrawal'. His analysis, which has value, leads him to conclude that social work can only be valid if it establishes much more modest goals and practice; he then seems to advocate the 'welfare secretary' role for the social worker. Such a response is evidently misplaced. While many discussions – those which confuse social work with social science and social service – would benefit by limiting the role ascribed to social work, Howe's proposal shuns the diversity and open-endedness which is the very strength of social work. It denies social work's capacity to explore experience, to be life-like. The problem, which is essentially one about the character of intuitive knowledge, leads Howe to a solution in which he turns his back on social work.

But perhaps the best illustration of the intellectual cul-de-sac into which current approaches to intuition lead social work is a thoughtful article by Brian Sheldon. In 'Theory and practice in social work: a re-examination of a tenuous relationship' (1978), he notes that theory and practice are, formally, barely linked; although it is the subject of frequent lip-service, their complementarity 'is part of a verbal rather than a real tradition in social work'. Sheldon points out that relating theory to practice is seen as a largely personal matter; he cites the phrase 'It all depends on what works for you' which social workers use so often when challenged to justify a particular approach. Sheldon, rightly, thinks this is an untenable state of affairs. 'It too easily leads to the spectacle of any three trained social workers deciding that any one client's problem is the result of either the suppression of his internalized "fun child", an upset in his family dynamics, or his hitherto unsuspected need for three days camping in Wales.' He objects to the uncritically eclectic knowledge base on which social work is said to rest (he calls it a 'knowledge pile'): 'new theories and new approaches are always possible if the logical relationship between existing contributions become too taxing ... Competing explanations must be made to compete.' This is excellent; social workers *should* be made to outline clearly the reasons for their assumption of a particular theoretical stance, and to identify the ways in which different theoretical positions account or fail to account for phenomena in the details of their practice. Such explanation will be taxing, but its conduct is essential for the welfare and development of social work. Equally desirable is the incorporation into common practice of a 'single case experimental design' procedure along the lines that Sheldon proposes, a procedure which requires the development of a critical attitude to each worker's workload.

But Sheldon, although he does acknowledge the essential intuitiveness of social work, does not give plausible account of its implications for these proper aspirations. He notes the ambiguity of judgements in social work; 'Our favourite adjectives are still "flexible", "intuitive", and "open ended", even though these are *partial* accounts of what is involved in social work practice' (my italics). Yet his conclusion is to emphasize only the rational part of social work: 'we could do worse than adopt the view that in some respects each of our clients is "like all other men, like some other men, and like no other man". Why can we not acknowledge that everyday practice is based as much on the two former categories as on the latter?' His article makes clear that there is no established way of dealing adequately with the intuitive element in social work, and that this intuition is a necessary feature of social work, but he then argues only for greater scientific-style rigour. Yet, as a necessary part of the whole, intuition cannot simply be set on one side as if it were theoretically inacessible, for it then wanders free, being held to no account, and appears at random to threaten and undermine the positivist approach which Sheldon advocates. Unless social work can show its workers the proper use of the 'idealist approach' (the term Sheldon adopts for an intuitive, phenomenological approach), social workers will continue to play low subjective trumps against positivist aces.

Sheldon tries to reduce the suspicion which he believes workers feel for a scientific approach by pointing out that all science is partially deductive and that hypotheses are made only by the taking of imaginative leaps: 'art and science, intuition and formulation, practice and theory, are [not adversaries but] related aspects of the same process of finding out and checking up on our beliefs'. This is a significant description which, as will be seen later, is a necessary step in the real recognition of intuition; it points to the relative importance of the two approaches and their necessary co-existence each with the other. But it does not explain *how* the worker establishes that 'disciplined use of self' upon which Bill Jordan (1978), commenting upon Sheldon's article, believes the worker must rely. Jordan emphasizes the importance of the worker's powers of communication, the emotional interaction between worker and clients, and even that social work is concerned with 'sharing, possibly with loving'; for these reasons 'ideas which stimulate the imagination, the sensitivity and self awareness of social workers may be just as useful as precise scientific formulae'. Jordan correctly notes that Sheldon's knowledge base gives no substance to these areas, and that their necessary inclusion means that social work can never be compared to plumbing or chemistry, as Sheldon apparently would wish. Sheldon's article thus illustrates particularly well the general difficulty posed by social work's emphasis upon intuition, for the mere acknowledgement of its persistent presence is not sufficient; an account of social work must incorporate a proper account of intuition. Indeed, Jordan's comment itself illustrates the problem, for that comment, while necessary, in fact only reasserts that perspective in social work to which Sheldon takes exception. Both authors purport to acknowledge the necessary place of the 'positivist' and the 'idealist', the rational and the intuitive, yet neither develops the two together. They face each other across a divide.

It is worth noting that Jordan (limited to a note of only three pages) does offer a real clue to the way in which this problem can be identified and resolved. He writes of Sheldon's analogy of social work with medicine.

> Much of what [doctors] do is not 'problem solving' ... at all. The best doctors recognize a human element in their practice which was brilliantly analysed in John Berger's book, *A Fortunate Man*. His description of the helping relationship between a country doctor and his patients is immediately recognizable to social workers. Berger makes it clear that his subject did not learn this side of his work at medical school; yet social workers should learn it in their training.

Indeed, social workers must achieve such learning in their training, although it is not currently clear either that they do so or that their training is properly organized to make such learning a reality. But the significance of Jordan's comment lies as much in the medium of his assertion as in its substance. His citation of *A*

Fortunate Man is entirely merited – it is a book of real relevance for social workers – but it is also important to note the form which Berger used to create this work and Berger's own credentials. Berger here writes a splendid form of imaginative documentary narrative, and is himself both novelist and critic; a novelist, moreover, whose creative work is sometimes distinctive because of the unusually deft way in which he combines theory and experience, the general and the particular. Jordan's citation therefore suggests not only the necessary professional qualities which Sheldon's account has omitted, but also something of the tradition in which an understanding of those qualities must be located.

CREEPING TOWARDS INTUITION

A particularly interesting discussion of the nature of social work's knowledge is to be found in Timms and Timms (1977), *Perspectives in Social Work*, in which the authors not only note the need for a disciplined and rational approach to social work, but also give a measure of detail as well as sympathy to an account of intuitive understanding. They do give substance to the necessity of developing both approaches. Nonetheless, despite their sympathy (and the considerable value of their general review), their account eventually founders upon the same obstacles as Sheldon's (1978) discussion of theory and practice; their acknowledgement of intuition is sympathetic but it is still insufficiently developed to make clear the practical implications of such an approach.

Timms and Timms analyse the nature of the social worker's knowledge, and they also discuss the suspicions of 'knowledge' which have been apparent in social work. They cite references to 'heart' and 'intuitive' knowledge. Goldstein (1973) is taken as an example; they quote a passage in which he writes of 'knowing in internal ways the inner state of others at times without the benefit of specific clues'; other social workers are said to give their material a similar emphasis. This leads the authors to conclude that there is in social work a preference for 'a particular way of knowing, that of personal experience of a kind that cannot easily be described. That which is elusive, that which is of the finest nuance, that which can only be "experienced" has always held a considerable attraction for social workers.'

Timms and Timms are evidently very uneasy about this emphasis, with good cause. Of Goldstein's intuition they comment that 'It is, of course, difficult to conceive of knowledge in the face of complete deprivation of any specific clues, and one is led to the conclusion that the intuition referred to is expected to do too much.' One concern, it should be noted, is apparently the degree of emphasis which seems to be placed upon intuition. They go on, however, to explain their more fundamental concern.

> If social workers are inevitably bound in by their subjective understanding of the subtleties of feeling there is no way of choosing between accounts and no way of improving one's understanding. We would be left with a group of people (social workers) who, relying on only personal insight, would be unable to converse on their understanding. There could be no possibility of transmitting systematic knowledge through training.

It *is* hard to conceive of knowledge without 'any specific clues'; such knowledge will apparently leave us without a way of 'choosing between accounts', and only constitute 'knowledge' according to a narrow definition of the term. But social work does rely, in part, upon something like such knowledge. Sometimes, write Timms and Timms, 'we know something because we – and only we – know we have decided something.' Such 'personal' knowledge extends beyond decisions; social workers must, for example, rely upon an awareness of their own past and current experience to inform their understanding of their clients. But such knowledge is not 'magicked' into existence; its origin can be traced and articulated, and at least partial descriptions offered. Such descriptions are 'partial' because they are never exhaustive; we can never entirely account for experience because of the infinite diversity of relevant thought and feeling, but we can locate important reactions and ideas. We have *some* clues, even if they are not precise.

Timms and Timms imply that we must use such clues, but give little idea how this can be done in any disciplined manner, even though they themselves point to the direction in which social work may find a solution to the problem. In effect, in this respect, they ultimately echo the status quo which they find insufficient.

They point to the tension in social work between the 'intuitive' and the 'rational'; they explain the necessity for social work to establish clearly that there are areas in which there must be rational debate and scrutiny, and they offer help towards this end by identifying that there are limitations on 'scientific' practice: 'it is clear that scientific activity is only one way of being rational and that it has no monopoly even if it has great prestige'. Their illustrative contrast, at this point, is between the scientist and the historian; they cite Popper to the effect that 'some disciplines are more interested in the universal statements and others in the statements concerning the specific situation'. Social work, conclude Timms and Timms, requires both 'explanation and understanding'. They define explanation as a 'scientific' concept along the lines of a general law, and understanding as the recognition of belief as a determinant of human action.

A differentiation along these lines, of explanation and understanding, is of crucial potential importance and plays a significant role in subsequent discussion. Its implications extend beyond the shift to a philosophical emphasis which the authors effect, important though this be. It requires that some framework be established which will enable social workers to be articulate and critical about personal experience. Timms and Timms, it is clear, do not in any way abandon the intuitive, even though they wish to confine it to its proper place; but they do not give adequate clues about the way in which it must be handled. They write that at times 'We understand because we see – and sometimes it is like seeing – that a person's behaviour is appropriate', and that 'Sometimes this understanding can only be achieved by imaginative effort.' But if effective social work must rest upon a discriminating ability to 'see' and to 'imagine', it will be necessary to do much more than acknowledge the importance of such activities. They must themselves constitute part of an explored and disciplined perspective.

Much of the continuing discussion in *Perspectives in Social Work* emphasizes not only the importance of clear thinking and analysis, but the extension of social work's intellectual attention to a much broader range of concepts than the psychological and, to a lesser extent, sociological fields to which it has usually been confined. These emphases are entirely to be welcomed; there is an evident need for such clear, disinterested thinking in social work, for Mathew Arnold's 'free play of thought upon our routine notions' to promote constructive criticism and the development of more relevant perspectives. Social work needs an adequately intellectual culture in which truly appropriate concepts and analyses can be carefully examined. Timms and Timms contribute to such an examination and their work is useful particularly because of its emphasis upon the 'nature of knowledge' in social work, a problem with which social workers must make themselves much more familiar. The clarification of this problem, it will become clear, is integrally linked to social work's proper grasp of the intuitive use of self.

But it is insufficient merely to *note* the co-existence of different modes of knowledge. If social work is not to be constantly undermined by its intuitive foundations, there has to be some much more substantial reckoning of the relative weight to be given to the 'intuitive' and the 'rational', and how they are to be handled relative to each other. Without the one, in social work, the other cannot stand; there is no way in which the matter can be given one-sided attention. The acquisition of knowledge must, it is true, stem from the recognition of 'clues'. Social work must, it is true, transmit systematic knowledge through training. But it will not be possible to counter the 'preference for a particular way of knowing' just by asserting the merits of another way of knowing. The need is to give to the 'particular way' of knowing some proper shape or form. Then social workers can be required to give intellectual account of themselves, fully 'to converse on their understanding', a task which many woolly-minded workers will, it is true, find very daunting.

It is incidentally (that is, incidentally to this specific argument, but by no means incidentally to the general problem of intuition) interesting to note a marked similarity between one passage of Timms and Timms and Jordan's previously noted allusion to John Berger's work. Timms and Timms write on the diverse elements within the client's world on which the worker may focus: 'social work can be seen as a series of actions guided by certain dominant pictures. In our view, the major rule to be followed has been simply stated in an altogether different context – only connect.' This reference is noteworthy in two ways, again because of its substance and its medium. In content, it points to the need to clarify the kind of activity implied by making 'pictures' and 'connections'. But the reference to 'only connect' points to the meaning and medium of E. M. Forster's novel *Howard's End*, in which the phrase 'only connect' is the *motif*. Like Berger, Forster was also a critic as well as a novelist, and he was frequently preoccupied with issues of personal understanding and maturity, and the emotional and intellectual integration it requires; his writing is of considerable relevance to social work. Timms and Timms do not discuss or develop this allusion, nor others made to literature elsewhere in their work, but it is clear that they, like Jordan, have to look to the tradition of imaginative writing to find proper expression for some of their understanding of social work.

But it is, curiously, a work which indicates no particular sympathy with the idea of intuitive knowledge, let alone literature, which makes most clear the need for social work to come to terms with its dependence upon intuition. In *Towards Practice Theory*, Curnock and Hardiker (1979) search for the character of an adequate 'practice theory' for social workers and examine carefully the way in which social workers use their knowledge in their work with clients. They show precisely, and empirically, the heterogeneity of the worker's knowledge, its selection and synthesis, and the active and exact use to which this knowledge is given. 'However much knowledge [the workers] had about criminal behaviour, NAI, behavioural problems or terminal illness, the workers had to rely on their own feelings and observations in order to come to a comprehensive and integrated conclusion about exceedingly complex situations.' They suggest that the practice theories which guide the social worker are 'made up of a combination of explicit theoretical knowledge, practice wisdom, feelings and observations. But the *process* by which all these ingredients are employed is little understood ...' The ingredients are used to form a 'unique blend', but 'the constituent elements in this "blend" have rarely been identified, let alone documented'.

It is evident that Curnock and Hardiker appreciate that 'making sense' is the central task of the social worker, and they offer concepts and procedures which help explain the task. First, they outline a concept of 'individualization', 'a way ... of finding out what [a client's situation and problems] mean to that particular person'. Secondly, 'ideologies', which are 'relatively abstract bodies of ideas, beliefs and interests which are systematic enough to portray an underlying attitude' constitute the constructs which social workers use to bring order to perceived phenomena. Both concepts are used in the context of 'interpersonal communication processes', and the whole is set within a problem-solving model emphasizing 'risk, needs, resources and goals'.

This model has obvious similarities with an emphasis upon meaning and understanding, and the concept of 'ideology' clarifies the way in which systems of ideas, beliefs and values will determine the worker's perception. The model also confirms the importance of the communication of understanding. But there is no suggestion that the authors would favour a concept of 'intuition', for their search is implicitly one that will continue to look primarily to the social sciences for a solution. Yet their work poses exactly those problems which the concept of intuition seems best suited to answer. The significance of their work is in the substance it gives to descriptions of social work which have before been easily scorned; Curnock and Hardiker see the processes of the selection and synthesis of knowledge and its exact communication not as whimsical ideas which should be dismissed, but as established practices which must be explored and explained. It may be unlikely that they would themselves settle for 'intuition' as a sufficient concluding concept, but the character and substance of their description makes it clear that social work's necessary 'practice theory' cannot be described in any other way.

Curnock and Hardiker's work is important for more than the outline of a description which seems to fit intuition well; it also confirms the nature of the problems and solutions associated with that description. The central problem is to get access to the subjectivity of the social work process. The authors illustrate the problem by comparing two different analyses made by probation officers; they note that they 'filtered a mass of data and made some sense of the situation by studying the offenders' respective offences in the contexts of their rather different personal and social situations ... It is impossible for anyone to know what swung the balance in these two cases.' But perhaps it is not altogether 'impossible'; the authors go on to liken their concept of practice theories to 'signposts':

one of the problems is that these signposts are rarely documented,
so that each generation of social workers has to work out its own
practice rules for itself. There will always be an element of
individual-working-out in social work practice ... However, it
may be possible to identify and document some of these signposts,
which can then be taught relatively explicitly to future gener-
ations.

It seems unlikely that Curnock and Hardiker's anticipation of
'explicit' practice rules will be realized, but their emphasis upon
documenting the detail of the social work process to overcome
the 'impossibility' of understanding subjectivity will prove to be
exactly the procedure required by the elaboration of the concept
of intuition. Such elaboration will require further discussion and
development but, at this stage, it is important to note that these
authors not only describe the necessity for a concept of intuition,
but also give credence to that description by confirming the
directions in which such an emphasis must lead.

But the words 'it may be possible to document' hardly have the
ring of a rallying cry; *Towards Practice Theory* gives some
precision to a familiar problem, but it does not itself offer the
solution. Its thesis is consistent with recognition of the fundamental importance of the social worker's intuitive use of self, but
it does not itself offer such recognition. Curnock and Hardiker
look over the edge, but fail to take the leap. Like other social
work theorists, they find it difficult to develop the implications of
their understanding.

No theory of social work has made adequately clear the
essentially intuitive basis of all social work practice. It has been
evident that social work has some persistent subjective content,
but this has been seen either as a somehow supplementary matter
of feeling by itself, or as an issue to be regretted and minimized. It
has not been properly shown as the root of social work's
professional knowledge and skill. This failure has profound and
persistent implications for the practice and organization of social
work, for it places social work in an impossible position. Social
workers experience a significantly 'idealist', intuitive reality, but
this experience has no properly identified or articulated form.
Social workers are given no confirmation of their experience, and
so that experience does not 'exist'. Instead, social workers are
exhorted both by theoreticians and managers to strive for domi-

nantly 'positivist' goals which, however worthy in themselves, must be unattainable because they are insufficient. It is a schizoid stance; small wonder then that the institutions of social work show constant signs of stress and strain.

5

The Urgent Problem of Good Practice

OBSTACLES TO GOOD PRACTICE

The use of intuition, of 'self', is an integral, essential element in social work practice; it is the medium which enables the worker to realize his knowledge and ability on his clients' behalf. But this same intuition is also persistently problematic in social work, uneasily accepted and inadequately developed in both theory and practice. This is a matter of the greatest importance because it makes it impossible for social work to develop any proper critical procedures, and thus to distinguish competent, genuinely helpful practice. It also explains other important, and related, issues: the apparent rejection of learned theory by social workers, the apparent difficulty social workers have even in describing what they do, and the evident difficulty there has been in establishing an appropriate organizational pattern for social work. These are the issues which are the focus of this chapter.

THE REJECTION OF THEORY

There has been considerable comment on the rejection of theory by social workers, and on their apparent 'anti-intellectual' attitude (e.g. Bartlett 1970, Carew, 1979, Tropp 1976). This doubt about the value of theory for practice is characteristic of many occupational fields; it is not just in social work that professional novitiates are told by their experienced colleagues 'to forget all that college theory'. But it seems that such an attitude is particularly true in social work. Indeed, it seems at times as if there is a suspicion of *any* thoughtful approach to practice, a suspicion which sometimes seems like an active hostility. It is as if it has become, in some circles, almost a matter of faith to renounce a 'theoretical' or analytical approach.

Foremost amongst the reasons for this state of affairs is the social work's *learned* suspicion about theoretical perspectives. Social workers are assumed, and taught, to base their professional understanding on material derived from the social sciences. But this material, it is now clear, cannot itself ever be a sufficient prescription for practice because of its general and abstract character. Without some understanding of this limitation, and of the personal processes of selection and synthesis, interpretation and integration, which are always necessary in the social worker's use of theory, such material cannot be relevant. But social workers are not usually taught this distinctive character of their knowledge, and so they quickly (and, by their available lights, rightly) discard their theory because it does not 'fit' – it offers no adequate match for the world which they find in practice. So it is the experience of many social workers in training that they are required to absorb a range of offered theory without real attention to its use, meaning and integration. Not surprisingly they do not therefore find it useful in practice. Thus much social work teaching in fact contributes directly to the sometimes intellectual aridity of social work. It is not the case, as will later be made clear, that social workers should be excused the need for theoretical and intellectual lucidity, but social workers do not recognize the distinctive discipline which their emphasis upon intuition must place upon their use of theory. Social work, wrongly, becomes atheoretical and anti-theoretical as a result.

THE PROBLEM OF DESCRIBING PRACTICE

Social workers find it notoriously difficult to describe their practice, to explain what it is they 'actually do'. There is no accepted or conventional procedure for giving accounts of practice. It is not, for example, *required* of intending social workers that they show themselves able to make account of their work; the assessment of competence is largely a matter for lone field-work teachers, and the national validating procedures do not make candidates for qualification submit accounts of their field-work for independent or wider scrutiny. This educational prac-tice in turn reflects agency practice; there is not any established fashion in which written accounts of social work by social workers show the range of factors considered, the assumptions which influenced their selection and interpretation, the analysis and strategy derived from them, and the nature and effectiveness of the intervention. Indeed, it is an unfamiliar and a difficult task for many (perhaps most) social workers to give such an account. Nor is it normally thought to be necessary; both the 'professional culture' (the opinion of the majority of workers) and employing agencies seem only to require a relatively simple narrative description of work events.

The absence of such a tradition, in a verbal as well as written form, makes it difficult not only for laymen to know the nature of practice, but for social workers themselves to discuss their practice. This absence reflects the difficulty which social workers have in conceptualizing practice. In the absence of any structur-ing theoretical framework they have to rely for guidance upon either conventional local practice (sometimes a version of agency procedure), or upon 'whimsical theory' – for example, that 'adolescent male delinquents should be supervised by a woman' (or by a man: the version varies) – which is not subject to any critical appraisal or further substantiation. This is the subjective confusion – 'anything goes' – which so many commentators find disturbing. But it is now possible to see that this condition results not from failing to strain after a scientific attitude, but from the *de facto* rejection of such an attitude. There is a lack of adequate intellectual scrutiny in social work, and its absence rightly undermines social work's credibility. But it is a difficulty which must persist until social workers find some systematic way to give account substantially to their intuitive use of self. Such account is a prerequisite to the subsequent and appropriate use of any more rigorous intellectual scrutiny.

This problem is illustrated by the experience of those able workers who can use frameworks which structure analysis and intervention, thinking and doing; who can do so because they have an ability to make good intuitive use of self. These workers cannot usually explain that this use of self is a necessary part of their work, for there is no shared professional language or theory which enables them to do so. They therefore give a partial account of their practice, purposeful but incomplete. Without prompting, it is still not clear how their work with their clients is effected, or even the detail of what has happened.

But such workers can be prompted, or drawn out in discussion; two things then become apparent. The first is that the full accounts which then emerge characteristically involve an initially diffident but later more fulsome account of their own past and present in the events described. For it is not possible to describe good social work without a proper account of the actor/narrator through whose eyes and mouth the account lives; without this account the matter is dead. Yet the account of this necessary self-involvement is gauche because it is not usually legitimated by the worker's frames of reference. Neither his theoretical nor his agency structure requires such an account of him; both acquiesce to the wider social convention which treats such accounts of emotion, perception and experience with suspicion. In asking workers to give such an account there is a resistance which has to be overcome, sometimes only with difficulty.

In such discussion it also characteristically becomes apparent that the good worker uses a distinctive style of language, one which is personal, evocative and imaginative. Good accounts of good social work are rich in imagery; they evoke the experience of those concerned; they use a range of colour and texture which are of necessity precluded in 'scientific' description. This is not the only style available to such workers, for they must also be able to give clear accounts of analysis and procedure; but it is *because* they can master the experience and the image that they can then give this analytic account. Yet such imaginative accounts do not conform to the available conventions of theory or bureaucracy. As a result the worker hesitates to offer such account and the necessary description is then denied.

When such accounts are given, it is striking how the worker himself often appears to change – revealing the enthusiasm and vitality which are a necessary facet of effective social work. This energy seems to be released almost with a sense of relief, for the able worker needs to be able to share his understanding and involvement. If he is to remain able, his own experience requires 'confirmation' as much as that of his clients' and it is only by such personal account that his experience is recreated to be made accessible. Yet too often such sharing occurs only by accident, or because of good support from friends or family – or not at all, to the cost of professional ability and well being. Social workers are not often required to give such account, in training or in work, and many are unaware even of the need to do so; as a result, they are unable to give adequate account of their practice for they do not know the form or the discipline which such account requires.

THE DIFFICULTY OF IDENTIFYING GOOD PRACTICE

Social work's confusion about the use of self and intuition makes it difficult not only to describe but to evaluate practice. The competent worker may have only some 'sense' of his own worth, a tenuous grasp which can be easily and inadvertently under-mined. It will be difficult for him to assert (even to himself) the value of his practice without any recognized language with which to do so. It will also be difficult for him to articulate or identify his misgivings. He cannot be clear about the nature of good practice, his own or other people's; he is indiscriminate about professional competence. Yet this is an unreal situation. We know from common experience that some people are more helpful than others, and that some people are very little help at all. It is not that workers believe, in reality, that there is no difference in the help that different people offer. Yet, professionally, social workers sometimes seem to deny even the possibility of distinction between the worth and work of their colleagues; they do so because they cannot adequately discriminate without a language and a framework which charts the necessary elements of their professional practice.

The result is not only the failure to recognize good practice; it is the proliferation of bad practice. Social workers, be they good or bad practitioners, are usually conspicuously well-meaning people, concerned for others and to do right by others. They therefore not only have the normal need for the security of purposeful activity, but that need is sharpened by their feeling for the distress which they routinely encounter. They *must* do something to help people; they must *do* something to help people.

Yet social workers cannot easily identify the appropriate and competent action, because there is no conventional recognition of good practice; even less then can they recognize that competent practice, because it depends so much upon understanding others and encouraging the activity of others, is often initially passive. Yet if understanding is the necessary prerequisite for effective action in social work and if its communication may often constitute *the* action, it must be a cardinal rule for social workers that they do not get in the way of their clients' coping efforts by the intrusion of their own activity. But the untutored and indiscriminate judgement of some workers, led by their necessary compassion, leads inevitably to activity even when understanding is confused – activity which may be entirely ill-judged. It is an old and familiar story, but it is still true; the well-meaning peformance of inappropriate tasks is the frequent characteristic of bad social work. But such bad practice cannot easily be countered in the absence of sufficient criteria for good practice.

THE PROBLEM OF ORGANIZING SOCIAL WORK

The appropriate mode of organization for social work is much debated. The pretensions of the social worker to be a 'professional' are disputed because of his failure to acquire an exclusive base of knowledge or skill, yet social workers have often sought relative autonomy within their agencies. It is the confusion about intuition which means that it is not generally clear what it is that social workers know and do. Agencies, nonetheless, have responsibilities which are relatively clear and defined, and some of them attract close public attention; agencies therefore must act to show that these responsibilities are responsibly and sensibly undertaken. Yet they must act in a situation in which social work itself is ill defined, and its practitioners may be either inarticulate about their practice or actually incompetent, for the absence of established criteria for both the description and evaluation of practice means that even if agencies employ qualified workers there is no guarantee that they will be competent.

It is not, therefore, surprising that agencies seek at times to organize work and workers so that social work is given some routine and uniformity. In the absence of plausible professional criteria and control there is no other apparent means to achieve reliable service. This need, in part, explains the distinct 'management' ethos which has recently become characteristic of so many British social work agencies, in which managers exercise control over significant aspects of the worker's day-to-day tasks. Such a 'management' emphasis is also a function of the size and responsibilities of the social services departments, and the general social *service* role which they fulfil; the agencies manage significant and scarce resources and these must rightly be subject to control to ensure their proper allocation to the greatest need.

But such a 'bureaucratic' style of organization is not an evidently appropriate style for social work, in which so much professional knowledge and judgement rests upon the worker's intuition and is thus only available to the worker. Nor is it evident that contemporary social work agencies are organized in a way which is conducive to good social work practice. The absence of an adequate account of intuition means that it is unlikely to be recognized as an element of professional practice within the organization, and thus that it is unlikely that any provision will be made to foster that use of self which it requires. Indeed, there is no reason within the organization's rationale why those who manage social workers should even be competent – and thus sympathetic – in this area; the widespread confusion of social work with social service responsibilities has meant that social workers are managed by those whose priorities are properly those of general social service delivery. Social work is thus often provided in agencies organized in ways which may be inimical to social work and in which the organizers, for quite proper reasons, may be professional non-competents.

This situation has very high risks. The worker, already faced with the possible incomprehension of his colleagues, works in an organization which gives him profoundly contradictory messages. On the one hand he is told that his clients need personal care, for this is the nature of the social work role, and such personal involvement necessarily requires an intuitive use of self. On the other hand, he is asked to be the agent of an impersonal corporation which retains significant powers of judgement and decision. The worker, because his help is such an essentially personal process, must also have personal recognition and support, yet he is denied that understanding which he knows determines each person's coping capacity, his own no less than others. This is the schizoid conflict; people are deemed to need care and support to cope with stress (this is the worker's brief) and yet people are denied that care and support (this is the worker's experience). In a schizoid conflict the subject is likely to withdraw; the worker is unable to deal bureaucratically with situations because they are not and cannot be uniform, yet he is unable to make proper use of the personal response which the work demands. This incongruous situation is one of the significant determinants of the low morale which now seems so often to characterize social work agencies; there are others, of course (currently, especially, those of economic stress), but this one issue is persistently and distinctively problematic for social work.

Organization for social work poses problems of immense complexity. The lack of adequate clarity about the nature of the social work task means that, in effect, neither social worker nor social work agency is clear about their role. Agencies must organize to meet public responsibilities, yet neither agency nor worker, in the absence of an adequate language and model, can see clearly the ways in which social work must be differentiated from the routine provision of other social services, and the ways in which certain patterns of organization are inimical to good social work. Indeed, agencies cannot currently properly distinguish competent practitioners to whom they could give autonomy if an appropriate organizational framework did exist. It is a double-bind: the agency must protect its interests by structuring the work, but in doing so it disables the competent worker and inhibits the development of truly articulate and accomplished practice. Fortunately the direction of some current change seems to be the right direction; the overdue move towards decentralized local offices is not only likely to meet the obvious need for accessible personal services but perhaps implies a measure of increased autonomy for local teams. This may make easier an exploratory shift in the present balance.

Social work's difficulty in giving proper theoretical account of intuitive knowledge and intuitive behaviour has very serious practical implications. It makes it difficult for social workers to retain or use their theoretical learning; it makes difficult even the description of practice; it makes impossible the general recognition and evaluation of good practice; and, inevitably after such problems, it obscures the development of appropriate patterns of organization for social work. To grasp the character of this professional intuition is a problem of the most immediate and central importance for social work; it is, in effect, an issue about the plausibility of the whole social work enterprise.

TOWARDS GOOD PRACTICE

The need for an adequate model of social work is pressing and practical. After the promise in the 1960s there now seems to be a possibility that social work may fail to deliver the goods; dissatisfaction is widespread and threatening. The centre of distress is currently the local authority social service and social work departments, though in time there may be a more muted crisis within the probation service as it seeks to resist the role of community custodian. Within the local authority services, social work morale is often low, and confusion about role and purpose often high. Beyond the local authority there seems to be a considerable public and official suspicion, a suspicion which appears to have been sufficient to prompt the government to sponsor an inquiry (the Barclay Committee; NISW, 1982) into the role and task of the social worker. After the crusading optimism of the Seebohm Report (Home Office, 1968) there is now real doubt about the fundamental, root value of social work, doubt that appears to be present almost as much within as without the profession.

The threat is a real one; current confusion and dissatisfaction may undo the progress towards good which can come from social work and which was envisaged in the Seebohm Report. That good has evidently not been sufficiently realized, and in consequence the whole fabric and potential of social work seems to be under review. It does nothing to mitigate that review that so many changes and stresses have occurred over the decade, that social work has been subject to such unreal criticism about its role in child abuse, that agencies have developed cumbersome management structures, that difficult social work roles have been filled by the newly trained and the untrained, that tasks have been allocated to social workers which are evidently not social work tasks, that agencies have been given increasing responsibilities with decreasing resources. These issues do nothing to mitigate the review because social work has not, over this period, been able to ward off or challenge inappropriate developments. It has been unable to do so because of its persistent difficulty in formulating an adequate model of social work on which to base any articulate challenge to misconceived change. Morale is low in social work not only because of threat, but because of the difficulty of knowing how even in principle that threat should be countered. The optimism of the Barclay Report perhaps offers some temporary relief from these difficulties, but the committee's failure to deal with the central problems of the character of social work mean that the real confusion must persist.

The need for a more complete model of social work is therefore pressing. But the need exists even without the pressure of current stress: it is needed to further social work's present development. It is unfortunate that these difficulties have made it hard to see that many of the changes of recent years have been advantageous, and that social work has made considerable strides towards a much more positive practice. The Seebohm Report was recognition of the potential coherence and integrity of social work. The significant theoretical developments in the years since its publication have been developments encouraged by the existence of a 'generic' social work which makes it possible to envisage a social work role being distinctly and separately identified. It has become much more possible to describe, without mystery, much of what social workers actually do, because the focus has been more easily directed towards social functioning and social work help, and not towards the broader contexts against which social work is practised. But this has not been a sufficient development. It has enabled social work to establish the potential for an independent identity, but it has also shown that much more theoretical work must be done if social work is adequately to shape its independence and to realize its potential social value.

The risk is that without a more sensitive identification of the nature of social work, its practice will remain at worst a largely random procedure and at best little distinguished from any other common sense problem solving. This would be a tragic limitation; social work in fact promises a considerable social good which is already close to realization. The groundwork has been done. Yet social work cannot progress until it can develop criteria which allow some hard practical questions to be answered. The problematic issues in social work remain the identification of the appropriate knowledge for social work, the criteria and procedures for the recognition of good practice in social work and the appropriate pattern of education and organization for such good practice. These issues are problematic because of the nesessary emphasis in social work upon intuition, upon intuitive knowledge and intuitive behaviour. An adequate account of social work must recognize this intuition, for without an adequate account there can be no good, and no bad, social work. At present there is no way in which social workers can recognize properly the subjectivity inherent in their work and learn to deal with its implications, and thus there is no coherent way they can promote good practice and counter bad. The need is pressing; it is the crucial need if social work is to survive and to fulfil its proper social role.

PART 2

Art and Criticism: A Different Tradition for Social Work

6

The Social Sciences: an Insufficient Framework

SOCIAL WORK AND THE SOCIAL SCIENCES

It is almost invariably assumed that social work is intellectually rooted in the social sciences – a child of sociology, psychology, social administration and others. This mixed parentage sometimes attracts scorn and scepticism, as well as those familiar pleas that a greater intellectual rigour be achieved by restricting social work's intellectual sphere of operation. The effect of the assumption is to limit and undermine attempts to explore the nature of social work; it in turn limits the scope to promote good practice and to challenge the constraints upon it. The assumption itself is hardly ever explicitly challenged (the implicit challenge is the dismissive attitude many social workers have to training); there may be debate about how the social sciences should define social work but not about whether they should do so. Yet this assumption is evidently incorrect.

There is a perennial problem in social work about what knowledge should underpin professional practice; this problem, it can now be seen, is inherently insoluble, for since social work's principal concern is the understanding of each person's coping behaviour, it will be evident that there must be an infinite number of sources of influence all differently converging in different individuals. The social sciences will inform the social worker's 'schemata', offering 'tools which help us to see, evaluate and respond' (Abercrombie, 1969). The worker will use available perspectives which best help him explain the phenomena he sees, and which best help him see the phenomena to be explained, and these perspectives may be derived from or influenced by the social sciences. They will not, however, be confined to the social sciences; the social worker's means of selecting and integrating knowledge, and linking theory with practice, are not 'scientific' procedures and they are not restricted to the insights of the social sciences — indeed, it is unlikely that they are even primarily dependent upon them. The social sciences play an important role in social work. Historically they constitute the intellectual spring-board which has led to many systematic social endeavours, and they offer significant means to the potential understanding and articulation of the social worker. But they cannot be the basis of social work, and social work's nominal confinement within them has been a consistent impediment to its development.

Our understanding of the world is constructed, but it is not a random construction:

> [There are] certain 'rules' or 'models', without which no human being can [understand] in the ordinary sense at all. In each individual, the learning of these rules, through inheritance and culture, is a kind of creation, in that the distinctively human world, the ordinary 'reality' that his culture defines, forms only as the rules are learned. Particular cultures carry particular versions of reality, which they can be said to create ... [Further] the individuals who bear these particular cultural rules are capable of altering and extending them ... (Williams, 1965)

The social worker's understanding must include those rules which his society and culture (including his professional subculture) deems most important; he must be alert to them and articulate about them. He must be party to that 'shared reality' which individuals have collectively negotiated. There is, of necessity, some current expression of a shared reality in social work, for without it there could be no intelligible institution of social work. The problem is that the shared reality takes on no sufficiently precise form. There are some general indications of the relevant knowledge to be found, for example, in CCETSW's 'Guidelines for CQSW courses' (which require that social workers show some understanding of, say, developmental psychology, or of bureaucratic organizations), or in general definitions of social work (such as the useful definition of Timms and Timms, 1977, that 'social work in any setting is a process of communication between equal persons engaged in attempting to resolve problems of loss and change'). Guidelines and definition are potentially helpful; but they can tell only so much and no more; they must still leave open huge avenues for interpretation about the exact material to be learned. For social work is not a precise activity; the rules are largely unwritten and shift with the meanings and motives current in society. It cannot be otherwise. Even to identify the available rules is therefore a matter of strenuous activity.

This vagueness, this intellectual 'softness', has been the source of endless self-searching and doubt in social work because of the assumption that social work should share the (sometimes) scientific aspirations of the social sciences. There has been a sense that the social sciences have been improperly and haphazardly ransacked (for example, Sheldon's description of the 'knowledge pile'), that neither the selection nor the use of the material has been scientifically pure. So social work, intellectually, has taken on an apologetic air. It has paid a high price for this apology, not only in its own largely misplaced sense of inadequacy, but in its consequent failure to commit its energies to the development of institutions and understandings which could properly handle the nature of social work. The intellectual vacuum has contributed directly to the organizational and practice difficulties which have so characterized recent social work, and the inflated respect for the social sciences has led to a neglect of other relevant areas of human knowledge and understanding. Indeed, it has been argued by Davies (1981) that it has also resulted in the quite inappropriate neglect of necessary practical or factual knowledge by social workers, and that this knowledge is of much greater importance. Davies argues that there is no cause to think that the study of the social sciences makes for better helpers *per se* – a claim made even though some social workers are still given on qualifying an award in 'applied social studies.' So it is of great importance for social work that its adherents cease to see themselves as failed scientists, and recognize that for social work the scientific endeavour has always been misconceived. The real task is not to insist on science but to understand the actual nature of social work's knowledge, and then to consider its implications for systematic practice.

This task may be somewhat easier if social workers learn that they may themselves have misunderstood the nature of the social sciences. Social work has been offered, and has implicitly accepted, a view of the social sciences as a positivist, scientific activity. But there are other views about the status of this knowledge: the material of the social sciences can be understood in a light which makes it much more accessible to social work, and far more consistent with the social worker's knowledge of human and professional experience. This view reduces the emphasis upon the 'scientific' status of the social sciences and, in the light of this perspective, they can come to assume a much closer affinity to the nature of social work itself. In other words, whilst it may well be that the social sciences as sciences can have only a limited value, their relevance and use to social work is more intelligible when it is clear that this scientific status may itself be somewhat misconceived. Indeed, it may be that they need a perspective which social work itself can best provide.

UNDERSTANDING AND THE SOCIAL SCIENCES

Social workers have explored too little the debate about the nature and status of the social sciences, fearful perhaps that without the *possibility* of 'real' knowledge there can be no adequate basis for their efforts. Certainly they should know something of this debate, in order to get an idea of the nature of their knowledge. It may not be easy to include 'epistomological studies' in social work courses but without their introduction in some fashion social workers have no intellectual context into which to place their basic studies. (The works of Timms and Timms (1977) and Sheldon (1978), cited earlier, offer some introduction to this discussion from a social work viewpoint.) In consequence, they subsequently reject their learning when it shows itself to be different in kind to their 'knowledge of experience'. They need to learn something of the status of their knowledge in order to see that it need not be useless or invalid.

Indeed, social workers can hope to find more comfort than may lie in the mere discovery of inherent constraints in a 'social' science. This is illustrated particularly well in a book by H. P. Rickman. In his *Understanding and the Human Studies* (1967) there is in fact not only confirmation of the existence of such constraint, but confirmation too of the value of social work's potential contribution to the social sciences. Rickman's concern is the absence in the social sciences (the 'human studies') of precisely that mode of diverse 'understanding' which, it is clear, is fundamental and familiar in social work practice. Rickman has no explicit concern with social work but his argument is one which is both relevant and recognizable to social workers. He seeks to examine the status and logic of knowledge in the social sciences; his conclusion is that they fail to reflect the real nature of human motivation and behaviour. Writing of psychology, he notes:

> The open minded empiricist contemplating the mass of expressions ... already available, though much of it has not been used by psychology because of the inadequacy of techniques and exploratory schemes available, will be struck by the complexity with which human life presents itself. What we encounter are not instincts, faculties, or general incapacities, but such concrete yet complex expressions as the ambition to get an interesting job in a rural area, or the pleasureable and yet shameful memory of an old love affair. Only when we have systematically accumulated evidence of this kind ... can we begin to draw theoretical conclusions and produce generalizations of intrinsic interest and value.

Rickman is clear that this complexity has to be seen as our common human nature.

Positivism, according to Rickman, has led to researchers choosing the easily accessible and avoiding the complex topics: 'we thus have precise knowledge of what is not worth knowing'; he dismisses the possibility of the human studies as a precise structure. 'The idea of the human studies as a tidy system starting from certain elementary insights and proceeding by logical steps towards comprehensiveness is a will-o-the-wisp, something of which we had better not even dream.' It is, in a way, strange that such an assertion is not already central for social work, for the determinist and totalitarian implications of the possible existence of a 'tidy system' are horrific, and essentially antithetic to social work's emphasis upon respect for the individual. The 'scientific' aspiration always sat ill with not only the experience but the ethics of social work. But the recognition that 'we cannot escape from subjectivity' does not lead Rickman to abandon all the trappings of objectivity; at the very least 'our conclusions in each case have to be related to a body of independent evidence'. He later notes that 'critical awareness and constant care is ... required if the necessary processes of selection and interpretation are to be distinguished from moral valuations which distort the evidence'. So it is no part of Rickman's argument that the human studies must be short on intellectual stringency. Indeed, he argues that it is their essential subjectivity which *requires* that the most careful attention be given to evidence and substantiation. But at root they will rest essentially and inevitably upon man's 'ordinary' understanding.

Rickman asserts that the distinctive study of man requires that we

> enter into, and understand, the mental processes by which he gives meaning to the world. We cannot know why a person becomes delinquent without understanding his fears, ambitions and interests and the customs and moral standards of his society. These are the subject of human studies ... [Facts in human studies] are the thoughts, feelings, and intentions of people expressed in physical acts. They are subjective in that they are always the states of a subject, what somebody feels, how somebody experiences a situation or how somebody sees the world ... We are dealing with interpretations of reality. That they take place is a fact and so is their nature.

Rickman's emphasis upon meaning is crucial; it is meaning which gives the human studies their whole distinction. In turn, the key to meaning is the process of understanding; the observer may observe, but the sights he sees and the sounds he hears are not the subject of his study. 'The real subject matter of the human studies is only found in the act of understanding', which is 'sympathetic insight into the mental life of other people'.

> [Understanding is] the primary cognitive process through which the subject matter of the human studies is given to us; it pervades these disciplines and is indispensable to them; its successful conclusion on the highest possible level is the goal of the human studies. This orientation towards understanding thus characterizes the disciplines concerned with man and distinguishes them from the physical sciences.

Rickman considers that understanding must be classed with such familiar procedures as observation, experiment, induction and deduction as a means to increasing knowledge. 'The use of scientific method in the human studies involves understanding at every stage.'

However, while the use of understanding may distinguish the social sciences from other fields of study, understanding is not peculiar to the social sciences; 'any scientifically stringent approach towards the real understanding of human problems', argues Rickman, 'must be based on the refinement of the complex cognitive processes through which daily experience becomes meaningful to us ... Understanding is a familiar process which enables us to orientate ourselves in ordinary life. It reveals meaning as sight does colour.' In other words, just as the social worker must use that common process of understanding by which he and all men make sense of the human world, so should the social scientist, and, just as the social worker must seek to extend and refine that 'ordinary' understanding, so must the social scientist. Rickman makes this quite explicit: 'The human studies must deepen and systematize the insights of commonsense if they are to achieve a substantial body of knowledge about man.'

There are very clear implications in Rickman's analysis for any study based upon a disciplinary approach. It is not enough merely to point out that each of the social science disciplines takes an abstracted part of reality to make its own study, that different disciplines may bring their perspectives to bear upon a common topic, or that each subject of any disciplinary study necessarily has other dimensions. It must be understood that disciplines are conventions, conventions which have been of considerable use, but only conventions. The convention has been developed only for a functional purpose and it may not be well suited to other purposes; for these an 'integrated approach' is required. The concepts of meaning and understanding are inherently multi-faceted.

A mechanical combination of disciplines is no substitute for an integrated approach. It is not sufficient ... to combine psychologists and social anthropologists ... into research teams – nor is it enough to edit psychological, historical and sociological studies in one volume. This may provide material but it is not a substitute for a comprehensive understanding of a human problem.

The present value of Rickman's analysis thus lies in the profound confirmation and potential it gives to social work. It confirms important elements in the social worker's own experience; it acknowledges the diversity of material which make up human comprehension and motivation, and recognizes the social worker's discontent with the unreality and limitations of social science. It also, by its emphasis upon the concepts of meaning and, particularly, understanding, offers to social work the opportunity to exploit that mode of understanding which social workers necessarily already use. His work therefore counters the erroneous but potent confusion, even guilt, that social work experiences because of its failure to acquire adequate scientific credentials, and it goes further by indicating a role for social work of immense social value, for social work must be at the forefront of those social institutions which try to realize understanding. His thesis confirms the appropriateness of an approach in social work which uses the social sciences, but is not constrained by an unrealistic expectation of a scientific procedure. It also frees social work – indeed, it requires social work – to be subject to an *appropriate* intellectual rigour which has been previously absent. It is almost as if the tables have been turned; social work may have as many insights for the social sciences as have those disciplines for social work.

A DIFFERENT PARADIGM FOR SOCIAL WORK

A distinctive 'human nature', in Rickman's view, is peculiar to the human sciences. By human nature he refers to:

> the constancy of certain general limiting conditions, of the human situation, a fixed range of potentialities and capacities, constant tendencies and universal patterns of mental life ... All men have sensations and feelings and go through the process of thinking. We all know what it is to have an intention, to perceive meaning in situations and to express it ... [We] all encounter typical connections in our mental life; we know that perceptions arouse memories and feelings give rise to desires ... It must be emphasized that we are familiar with all this, not because we are engaged in psychological research or probing self analysis, but because we are men.

This description is inextricably linked to his concepts of meaning and understanding; it is also clearly a description of those same processes which constitute the essence of social work — of selection and synthesis, of meaning and perception, of understanding and action. So social work knowledge requires an adequate emphasis upon some concept of 'human nature', for without such emphasis there will be no development of coherent social work theory and consequently practice. Yet social work has no concept for this, the kernel of its work, and Rickman makes it clear that it cannot expect to find such a concept in the social sciences. Is social work's knowledge and understanding therefore something which is theoretically *sui generis*?

This is hardly likely. Social work, for all that it is a *much* more important activity than has generally been recognized, is not a new activity and does not use new knowledge. Its knowledge and practice stem from the understanding and helping that is common to all people. It is a familiar activity and the models for its knowledge and practice will also be familiar. The social sciences have not offered a sufficient model, although they remain central to social work; social work should therefore consider the likely value of the complement of the sciences, of the study of the arts. Rickman certainly suggests that the arts have potential for increasing our understanding of human nature; he notes, for example, the value of biographies and imaginative literature, commenting that 'in such works we sometimes recognize the familiar, sometimes become more clearly aware of what we know only dimly and sometimes, with a shock of revelation, gain fresh insight into our own human nature'. Can the arts therefore offer a paradigm for knowledge and practice in social work?

There is already detectable a suggestion that they may do so in the literary references in Jordan and Timms and Timms (see above, Chapter 4). Jordan in particular is explicit, for he not only refers to imaginative work, but writes that 'literature and poetry often afford far more penetrating and meaningful insight into the human heart than psychological texts' (Jordan, 1978).

Indeed, there are considerable references to art and social work in the social work literature. But almost invariably they make reference to social work as an 'artistic' activity, and then fail, as do those just cited, to develop the idea or to give it theoretical attention. Yet there are accessible accounts from literary theory which suggest that it may well be possible to sustain just such a link. Consider, for example, the striking conceptual similarity (not, alas, a similarity of language) between those concepts of meaning and of synthesis and selection which have been offered as the principal constituents of social work understanding, and this passage from Shelley's *Defence of Poetry*:

> Man is an instrument over which a series of external and internal impressions are driven, like the alterations of an ever changing wind over an Aeolian lyre, which move it by their motion to ever changing melody. But there is a principle within the human being ... which acts otherwise than in the lyre, and produces not melody, alone, but harmony ...

A later passage notes that 'All things exist as they are perceived; at least in relation to the percipient. "The mind is its own place, and of itself can make a Heaven of Hell, a Hell of Heaven."'

Shelley in fact uses the term 'synthesis' to describe the organizing principle within the human being. It is evidently the very same process that underpins the 'intuitive knowledge', the understanding, of the social worker. Thus the poet, like the social worker, derives his understanding from the procedures and premises of 'common' sense, of meaning. Raymond Williams, who cites these passages of Shelley in his discussion of 'the creative mind' in *The Long Revolution* (1965), discusses the view that such synthesizing is an ordinary human process, but that 'to be a poet is to carry to its highest form this general activity'. William refers to the work of the biologist J. Z. Young, in particular that 'The brain of each one of us does literally create his or her own world'. The poet therefore strives for the most (literally) meaningful understandings, the 'highest form' of harmony, of making sense.

The social worker is professionally committed to making sense, both of the client's perception and of his own understanding, which he must offer to the client; his own understanding, for his client's sake, must be no less than of the 'highest form'. He must find a perception which can extend that of the client, which can, in Shelley's words, 'withdraw life's dark veil from before the scene of things'. Is there then a sense in which the social worker is to be seen as a poet, as an artist?

7

Art in
Social Work Theory

INTRODUCTION

There is no developed theory of social work which incorporates a
theory of art. If there were, social work would not continue to
find the problem of subjectivity so consistently bewildering.
There are, however, substantial references in the literature which
give credence to some idea of social work as art. The majority of
these pay only cursory attention to this issue; they confirm a
possible link, but do no more. A few seek to develop further the
place of art in social work, but almost without exception they fail
to bring forward the theoretical and practical implications which
must inevitably follow from the location of social work within
the tradition of art.

ART AS AN ESCAPE FROM INTELLECTUAL DIFFICULTY

Many of the references to art in social work imply no more than a
passing recognition of a possible link, as if the idea of art is itself
as embarrassing, in this context, as the subjectivity which
prompts the reference. Art is understood to be an expedient way
of dignifying knowledge or skill which is clearly non-scientific,
but yet is nonetheless – in some usually inexplicit way – seen as
being coherent rather than haphazard. The significance of such
writings lies not in their theoretical elaboration, for in this respect
they have none and claim none, but in the implicit recognition of
the relevance of art as the means of explaining subjectivity in

social work. The problem of such writings is that they attempt to dismiss subjectivity; the difficulty is 'consigned' to art, but without development this represents little advance on those writers who deal with the problem by ignoring it. Without elaboration and incorporation of social work's subjectivity, which a recognition of social work as art will permit, the status of the principal argument is inevitably undermined.

Tropp's (1976) article also offers an illustration of this process. He writes of the need for social work to become systematic and scientifically vigorous: 'if we can specify – like chemists – what the components of a single knowledge cell are, we are then in a position to begin to connect these components'. Tropp clearly sees science as the desirable paradigm for social work, and believes that social work must edge towards it. 'As we solidify our knowledge, we move from pure art, which cannot be questioned as to "how you get from one point to another", to an artistic science – so that we can indeed answer reasonable questions.' He proposes a residual role for art as the skill which social workers will use in the application of systematic, scientific formulae. It is clear that the major problem for social work is the definition of these formulae; this is the area for study and analysis, for clear thinking. The application of these formulae is a matter of 'art', and as such does not require attention – indeed, it is not amenable to attention, for it 'cannot be questioned'.

Tropp's construction therefore recognizes art as some sort of 'intuitive skill', at the same time presenting it as something which social work must always strive to minimize as much as possible. His argument is already familiar both in his very proper plea for greater intellectual rigour, and in his disregard for the theoretical and practical consequences of its predictable non-attainment. Social workers will not long strive for any available intellectual exactness if they get no help to deal with the inherently unrealizable nature of 'science' in social work. Learning is not encouraged by unexplained frustration. Tropp's article posits a divide between theory and practice, and implies that one is intelligible and the other not, that one is scientific and the other artistic. He thus uses 'art' as a device for dealing with subjective imprecision, but does so implicitly; he does not examine the nature of art, of this particular art, or of the implications of deploying art within his model. He is moved, understandably, to use the concept of art because of the difficulties he finds in maintaining a scientific approach. But by failing to give the concept adequate attention his view of social work 'science' is left unchallenged; he reaffirms (his denials notwithstanding) the fallacious model of a positivist social work.

Art does not play a central role in Tropp's argument; it fulfils a residual role. But because it does have a specific place in his structure it indicates with some clarity the role that recurrent references to art have fulfilled in social work writing. Such references elsewhere may be bald and brief; for example, Richan and Mendelsohn (1973) note that, in social work, 'the art ... involves learning to handle ... feelings'. Such references may also be vigorous and imaginative; Claude Wiegand (1979) has already been seen to liken the social worker to the sculptor 'having freed the sculpted form from the marble' when he helps a client fulfil his potential. It is clear to Wiegand that these social work processes 'are the work of an artist as well as a scientist'. These authors have rather different views of social work (which may colour the style of their description); they make use of art though in much the same residual fashion as does Tropp. For these authors, and for others, an idea of 'art' is used casually as a vehicle for disposing of the obvious and imprecise subjectivity of social work. Yet without elaboration such references give no better purchase than any other means of fumbling with that subjectivity, and without a purchase there is no means of assessing the implications of that subjectivity for *all* social work. By shelving the problem the whole inquiry is rendered void. But the interest of these present references is to note that it is an idea of 'art' which has often served as a significant siphon for impenetrable theoretical problems in social work. Theorists have often cast a glance in art's direction, even though very few have attempted to explore the path. In doing so, by making reference to art, they have confirmed their recognition of an essential element in social work, and acknowledged too that it lies beyond the perceived terms of their own inquiry.

There exists, then, preliminary evidence that some social work theorists have noted incidentally the potential relevance of art to social work. By way of postscript it can be seen that a form of the reverse is also true. It is not unexpected that theorists of art should assert art's profound relationship with social life and its influence upon those 'capacities and resources of a person which are determinants of social behaviour' (Gotshalk, 1962); indeed, this relationship is at the centre of much of the argument of this chapter. But Gotshalk, one such theorist, later notes a much closer connection to the detailed focus of the present inquiry.

> In great art, experience and thought and energy and purpose are employed with precision, tact and a fine sense of form to bring forth a product radiant with immanent values. Now something of this sort is equally possible in all the major activities of living. All these activities can be purposively shaped so that they yield an intrinsic good and possess an immanent value ... [Especially] in professional undertakings and personal relations, some of the aim of fine art is clearly relevant.

Gotshalk was not discussing social work directly but, as a 'professional undertaking' resting for much of its effect upon 'personal relations', social work is a particularly apt example of the validity of his assertion.

NOTING THE SIMILARITIES BETWEEN ART AND SOCIAL WORK

A small number of social work writers have paid *explicit* attention to the parallels between art and social work, sometimes very briefly, but attempting to do more than designate an unexplored solution to a problem. These allusions to art are almost entirely 'instrumental' allusions; even where the theme of the work is in some way focused upon 'art and social work' the value of the link is seen to be only that it can in some way meet a specific purpose. These specific issues offer substantial confirmation of the integrity of social work in art, not because they offer any broad theoretical development but because, piecemeal, they constitute some recognition of the elements which contribute to such a theory.

Bowers, in a series of articles first published in 1949 (and reprinted in 1972), assembled for review a long list of definitions of social casework. He noted that before about 1930 definitions frequently described casework as an art, though it is not clear that these references were in any way developed. After that date writers attempted to develop more systematic descriptions in which the term 'art' would have no place. This was not a view shared by Bowers himself, who concluded his review with his own defintion emphasizing casework's status as an art, an art which made use of the 'science of human relations'. He also quotes approvingly a description by Mary Richmond which makes the same distinction between 'scientific mindedness and the artist's practised skills' which merge, 'as in all creative people they must merge'. By implication, art is the practice skill – a familiar description, albeit one which is here more explicitly and positively made. Bowers was evidently aware of the related theoretical issues, though they were not completely integrated; the burden of his own argument is to emphasize the development of a science of human relations which will see 'the individual as he actually exists here and now, with his hopes and fears, his satisfactions and his insecurities, his aspirations and his encumbrances'. Bowers deplores the tendency to departmentalize the individual among specialists, 'losing that rounded view'. Bowers thus offers both an emphasis upon art and a linked theme of seeing man whole; indeed, he also briefly suggests that it is as artist that the social worker can synthesize disparate material and employ it in specific, unique instances. But his emphasis upon a *science* of human relations has the effect of masking the importance of these insights; art is somehow still just indefinable practice skill.

It is, in part, because literature does study the whole man that Elizabeth Irvine (1974) addressed the theme of literature's special relevance in the study of social work; she notes that in literature it is possible to escape the 'abstractions' of economic, psychological or sociological man, and to 'observe him in his natural habitat'. She also notes the parallel, that the author writes as a whole man, so that literature is in some way an encounter between whole persons. In social work education, the use of literature is therefore more likely to encourage a necessary personal synthesis of material than are 'conventional methods' of teaching. She further notes of some social work writing that it has a descriptive, colloquial character which 'fits the nature of the material rather than the demands of scientism'. Irvine thus draws attention to a number of characteristics relevant to the place of art in social work, in particular, social work as an encounter between persons, the integration of knowledge and the 'ordinariness' of some social work descriptions. But she does not develop these themes to emphasize either their importance in social work practice, or the impact they must have upon any social work theory which incorporates them.

The principal focus of Irvine's attention is the relevance of descriptions of particular themes in literature for social work studies, especially psychoanalytic studies in social work; she sees these writings as complementary. The main burden of her papers is to cite examples which suggest that literature and social science are consistent, and then to urge that the literature may be the most convincing means of grasping the shared truth. But although Irvine asserts at one point that creative literature may contain some sort of superior understanding, the effect of her paper is to imply that literature can illustrate best the material of social science. Irvine hesitates to develop the implications of her theme; she notes not only that the insights of the creative artist are well formed, but that they obviously often preceded in time the formulation of insights in the social sciences. But she does not then go on to speculate on the sort of consciousness which made the artist's insights, and its general relevance to social work, although these questions arise directly out of her assertions. Instead she remains bounded by her social science framework and observes that the authors themselves would have better understood their characters with the aid of psychoanalytic theory. This observation misplaces the emphasis to which Irvine's sensitivity to literature gives access; her paper effectively points to the ways in which literature 'confirms' social science, rather than the other way around. It is obviously interesting to speculate on a potential increase in an author's understanding, but the most relevant question for social work concerns the structure and procedure of the understanding that the author *has* achieved already.

In her paper Irvine is tempted by theoretical extrapolation, but she resists temptation; despite her sympathy for literature she makes, in effect, little more use of it than suggesting it offers a supply of 'real' characters and situations, a form of case or project history. Literature becomes a 'quarry' of illustrative examples of insights. This is the use of literature proposed by a number of social work writers. Some of them are evidently people with a considerable breadth of knowledge of the arts and a profound capacity for response; their understanding is rich and sensitive, and art is an intimate part of its structure. Their view of art, in other words, appears in no way two dimensional and they clearly feel it has an urgent relevance for social work. Yet without a revision of their understanding of social work itself, their use of art (usually in teaching social work students) is inevitably constrained; the 'truth' of the artist – which may be more vivid or intelligible than other truths – is for them confirmed by the extent to which it illustrates defined theory. Used in this way literature is then only a support for other perspectives on human life; it is not, despite the intentions and sensitivity of those who propose such use, accessible as something of intrinsic value. This use of literature is of course a possible use in social work, or any other field, but it offers no access to the principal benefits which can be derived from the study of the arts.

The most obvious expression of 'literature as quarry' is in the preparation of literary extracts or reading lists which are intended to illustrate particular themes primarily studied as social science subjects. There are collections of literary readings prepared for their relevance to psychology or sociology. Coser (1963), for example, prepared a volume from many fiction sources which illustrated issues commonly studied in sociology. He noted in his introduction that literature can 'clothe the dry bones of social theory with the living and plastic tissue which grows from literary imagination'. It is not his purpose to explore the nature of the difference between sociology and literature, and there is no need to dispute his assertion that 'literary insights cannot replace scientific and analytic knowledge, but it can profit them immensely'. But social workers must notice his reference to 'living and plastic tissue'. Social workers do have to grasp and create such vital plasticity, so it must become their purpose to undertake such exploration. Coser only notes that literature may have many purposes other than such illustration but that, as a social scientist, they are not seen as his professional concern.

Probably the best known such material for social workers is not a compilation of readings but a bibliography, Clare Morris's *Literature and the Social Worker* (1975). Morris's collection is of considerable value as a basis for guided reading; she herself notes the difficulty and violence implied by categorizing fiction by subject, but any list which helps suggest and group themes treated in literature must be of immense value despite its inherent imprecision. On a more general plane Morris, in her brief introduction, finds herself in Irvine's dilemma; she notes the rich potential understanding that the student can derive from literature, but she gives emphasis to the use of literature for those less able to handle formal educational approaches, or for those who have not the time to undertake complete studies. So there is still an air of apology, or at least of diffidence, about the value of literature in formal study for social work; there is still a reluctance to assert clearly the inherent value of art.

There have been too few forays into the field of art in social work for this diffidence to stem from reaction to such explorations; rather the sense must lie in the general priority given to a positivist approach to the social sciences, and thus to social work. But even the current gentle movements have attracted some disapproving attention. The Association of Teachers in Social Work Education (1980), for example, noted in their comment upon proposed new guidelines for assessment in social work education that art could only ever illustrate the individual instance, and that the interpretation of an arts illustration 'traded upon' social science knowledge. The description (as in previous examples) may be a true, albeit an insufficient, account of the use of arts-based material; the significance lies on the slightly disparaging use of 'traded upon', and the failure to appreciate the necessity of learning to handle individual situations in a job in which all situations are partly individual.

O'Hagan (1981) has also noted the use of literature as illustration in social work education (and he noted its claimed value for offering general insight and engendering hope), as well as the frequency with which social work writers cite or quote literature. He disapproves of this use, however; far from believing that it is essential that such references be made, he considers that such illustration and emphasis upon literature are harmful. It seems, in O'Hagan's view, to detract from the possibility of presenting full and objective accounts of clients, and in any case casts little light upon the reality of *client's* lives, which he believes are cast in a different mould to those of the 'heroes' of literature. It is perhaps not surprising that O'Hagan thus fails to ponder on the inevitability of literary references in social work, for it does not appear he has been asked to consider art and social work as linked phenomena; nor, by implication, has he recognized the inherent inability of the social worker to collect or present enough 'objective' information to satisfy the demands of his desired objectivity. But O'Hagan's principal conclusion seems peculiarly sad and peculiarly false, for one who has apparently earlier studied literature: the suggestion that in literature and in life people are divided into central, heroic and flat, peripheral characters implies either poor appreciation or poor art. Raymond Williams (1965) has said of realist literature that, at its best, realism (which has a special relevance for social work) is about the interplay of centres of diverse consciousness; any periphery is thus only the edges of that selection necessary to make manageable our understanding of the world.

There are in fact real cautions to be observed in the use of literature as illustration. Perhaps O'Hagan's qualifications stem from the risks of 'poor appreciation' which may be inherent in trying to make such a limited use of material. For if there is no attempt in the use of literature to note its intrinsic value, rather than its value to illustrate other perspectives, it is not a use but an abuse of literature, for it denies that intrinsic value and wastes the profound available potential. Something of the nature of art's intrinsic value, something of the nature of 'good appreciation', will be explored in the following chapters. But it is important to be clear that any appreciation of literature (and of social work) must be critical and personally involving. F. R. Leavis (1962), in a paper entitled 'Sociology and literature', explained that:

> to conduct a profitable argument about the 'sociological medium of literature' you must have a more inward acquaintance with the works of literature from which you argue than can be got from a literary history or a text book . . . . [No] use of literature is of any use unless it is a real use; literature isn't so much material lying there to be turned over from the outside, and drawn on, for reference and exemplification, by the critically inert.

It is evident that many of those writers who have explored the links between art and social work have had a sense of this need for an 'inward acquaintance'. They see the value of literature to lie partly in the greater sensitivity and awareness of others which it promotes. Their account can usually be seen to emphasize, or at least to imply, the importance of an understanding which uses imagination and ability to select and to synthesize. So there is recognition of the need for a distinct personal consciousness; literature in particular is seen as a counter to the 'dehumanizing' effects of theory, including, alas, those of current social work theorists (Breen, 1981). But the actual scope of much of this writing is limited. Irvine's (1974) paper, for example, illustrates one rich potential use of literature in social work, and suggests some general points of principle along the way, but she does not develop theory or derive practice (in this case educational practice). The same is true of Moore's (1975) paper on the classroom use of Canadian literature. He introduces his work with very brief reference to a number of those issues which lie at the centre of the problem of subjectivity in social work: imagination, emotion, the link between the general and particular, the integration of theory and practice. His paper thus offers confirmation of the relevance of an 'arts model' of social work to key aspects of social work's subjectivity. But it does so almost implicitly; he notes these theoretical issues in social work and asserts the value of literature in this context, but then focuses discussion only upon the classroom use of literature and literary approaches. He does not develop the necessary implications of such use for social work's general theory.

A number of authors have thus noted the similarities of art and social work, and have given some initial recognition to the scope for a theoretical and practical framework based upon this similarity. There remains a need to develop this recognition, in theory beyond the general recognition of a need for a certain consciousness, and in practice beyond the use of literature as an instrument in social work education. But very few social work theorists have sought to establish a more developed framework.

TOWARDS SOCIAL WORK AS ART

A small number of social work theorists have given specific attention to the theoretical relationship between art and social work. Their work does not, in the main, look to theoretical or critical approaches to art, but they do provide explicit confirmation of the relevance of art to the problems of subjectivity and consciousness in social work. They are seeking to deal with familiar problems.

Elizabeth Irvine's paper on literature in social work education was preceded by a more explicitly theoretical paper about helping as an art. In 'Education for social work: science or humanity' (1969), she notes the limitations of a scientific approach to the study of man, fearing that it must exclude all that cannot be reduced to statistics. Art, which makes man the subject, is an 'antidote' to science, in which he is the object. Literature offers 'just those insights which are needed to preserve our concept of the fully human, of man and his dignity. We can learn a good deal about mental illness from the text book; there are things we can learn better from Shakespeare, Ibsen, Dostoevsky and Conrad.' But even in this paper Irvine does not much develop this belief in literature's ability to deal with the whole man. Yet the later (1974) paper does contain an observation which (although a subsidiary point) is particularly worthy of development. There she notes on a number of occasions that it often proves to be essential for helpers to adopt a narrative, even a poetic, style. She first notes Frend's curiosity that his own accounts should read like short stories; she cites Winnicott's description of the early experience of the child; and she notes of a narrative-style passage of Caplan (on pregnancy and marriage): 'This is good clear writing which fits the nature of the material rather than the demands of scientism.' The 'nature of the material' is presumably that concept 'of the fully human, of man and his dignity'. This appears to be the same 'nature' that Rickman defined as 'human nature' (see above, Chapter 6). Irvine's observation seems therefore to offer an elaboration of Rickman's view of the relevance of art; that something in the style, the form itself, of narrative or poetry is necessary adequately to represent man.

Whan (1979) writes of 'Accounts, narrative and case history'. His concern is not focused on the arts but he does emphasize the importance of 'the story' as a significant form. He notes that the story is the common way of recounting (biographical) experience, that it requires a temporal dimension which is not necessarily present in abstract accounts and that it offers a 'genre' of presentation which helps people link themselves to their culture. Whan's concept of 'story' suggests a vehicle which can sustain 'composite meanings' – how we give an extended or elaborated account of ourselves which must include many linked meanings. The implication must be to emphasize the importance of the worker as 'artist', as critic and creator of 'story', for the worker will have to have both a quick grasp of stories, and a fluent ability to construct them.

Some part of Noel Timms's work on the nature of knowledge in social work has already been discussed. His recognition of its diversity and the role of understanding was foreshadowed in an earlier lecture (1971) '... *and* Renoir *and* Matisse *and* ...'. In this paper he refers to the 'close and fruitful connections between literature (including literary criticism)' and social work. The reference is of interest partly because of Timms's inclusion of literary criticism; he thus acknowledges not only the insights of literature but their distinct nature which requires for examination a distinct analytical approach. Timms's subsequent emphasis is upon a model of 'practical philosophizing', which has much similarity with an emphasis upon social work as art. He notes the importance of the concept of 'meaning' (and of 'reality') and claims that attempts to understand it are essentially philosophical. He makes a plea both for a wider intellectual base for social work and for a more disciplined intellectual attitude to whatever knowledge is used in social work. But, despite his title (which he explains is a reference to a novel by Iris Murdoch), he does not develop the literary or arts analogy; his work (in this and later writing) has parallels to a 'philosophy of art', but he does not examine whether a critical approach to art identifies potentially useful critical approaches to social work.

A closer integration has been made by D. A. Millard (1977) in an article on 'Literature and the therapeutic imagination'. Millard, like others, is led to conclude that social workers must make greater use of literature, but he reaches this conclusion only after making comparison between the imaginative demands of both pursuits. Millard is very clear that effective social work is only possible with a certain quality of consciousness. He notes that in social work

> an empiricism uninformed by sensibility is the first step towards a technological sterility. And it is precisely because he has often failed to articulate an appropriate relationship between imagination and knowledge that the social worker is likely to find himself mystified by his own behaviour.

Millard goes on to explain that this failure of sensibility in turn leads to an increasing emphasis upon bureaucratic roles; he notes that social workers have no knowledge base of a scientific nature, and that an adequate sense of role must therefore be either a matter of personal identity or of bureaucratic identity.

In fact, of course, as Millard makes clear, social work cannot be a matter of bureaucratic role; it requires the quality that he terms the 'therapeutic imagination' – a quality that is obviously a central facet of the pervasive subjectivity in social work. His comparison with the literary imagination is sustained by reference to literary criticism and theory; he examines the nature of the artist's knowledge, and sees that it is immediately relevant to social work. The problem is to develop (and he might have said to identify) such imagination, for 'it demands the cultivation of a particular sensitivity and we have not as yet been clear how this might be done'. There is, it will be seen, ample confirmation in literary writings of Millard's view of the nature of this sensitivity, and there is no reason to challenge his belief in literature's varied value; he believes in particular not only that it will widen experience, but that it clarifies necessary questions about morality and cultural identity. Millard's paper thus offers both a substantiated basis for a use of literature and a diversity of possible advantage, but his answer to his own question about the means of extending sensitivity is confined to the promotion of a wider use of literature in social work. This conclusion is reaffirmed by Margaret Valk (1979a) in a comment on his paper. In addition she points out that literature (and she also includes the use of criticism) is particularly helpful in exploring the inherent ambiguity of 'reality'. Literature is important to help achieve sensibility, for otherwise, in her view, its achievement must await the passage of time and 'meaningful experiences with clients and others'. Thus for both authors art, through the use of literature, can increase sensibility, but its value is in fact still confined to such use.

A much more developed view of social work as art is available in Lydia Rapoport's 'Creativity in social work' (1968). Rapoport's concern in this paper lies not in the use of literature or other arts to widen the sensitivity of social workers, but in the general similarities between the social worker and the artist. She perceives a quality of 'creativity' in all good social work, and believes this attribute must be central. Her essay explores the common features of art and social work to see what light can be shed upon this creativity. She notes that in general society art is regarded with suspicion and that in the social work literature it is 'only given a nod'. She also asserts that social work is 'rooted' in the scientific approach but that, while science describes the formulation of knowledge, the adaptation and application of its principles is 'an artistic task'.

Rapoport's account of the common nature of social work and art recognizes the characteristics which have identified the problem of subjectivity in social work.

> [Both social work and art are] engaged in problem solving, be it the problem of expression, communication, transformation, or change. Both deal with human materials or human themes and both require an intimate 'knowing and contact'. Both call for creative and imaginative use of self. Both require a special kind of distance and objectivity.

She notes in particular four common elements. First, the 'creative impulse' which is required to bring order out of chaos; then 'imagination', which she describes as 'thought content that is divorced from its perceptual origins' and is central to empathy and innovation; then 'intuition', which is perceptual rather than conceptual knowledge and thus, at the time at least, enables us to make judgements without knowing how we arrived at them; and, finally, 'style', which refers to the structure which the worker imposes upon his work. In this account Rapoport described 'insight' as a product of imagination and intuition.

These elements are clearly intimately linked to the characteristics of subjectivity discussed in earlier chapters. In particular, creative impulse and, to a degree, style reflect the 'meaning' which each person, and each worker, must impose upon the situations he encounters. The immediacy of much social work knowledge is recognized in the description of intuition. The empathic, imaginative quality essential in the social worker's understanding is seen as an integral part of his ability. Rapoport gave additional emphasis to the concept of 'meaning' earlier in the paper; she wrote that: 'art involves the communication of meaning ... [and] provides for a quality of experience'. Rapoport thus confirms the central importance of subjectivity in social work; indeed, elsewhere (1960) she wrote 'what we do is what we are' – a view which, it will be seen, closely matches a theory of literary creativity which is immensely relevant to social work. But Rapoport does more than confirm the central importance of subjectivity; she gives it shape by drawing on the comparison with art. She thus gives explicit confirmation to the idea that in art social work will find not just some instrumental use but a general model whereby to guide its practice. Art may do more than help extend 'sensibility'; it may help us understand its nature.

Any such development must have implications for practice as well as for theory. Rapoport gives some initial indication of these. Chief amongst them is her description of 'style', that 'it is possible to apply some principles of aesthetics to a given piece of social work practice' and that we do sometimes describe work with terms such as 'beautiful'. It is not necessary to accept Rapoport's contention that the primary property of beautiful work lies in its sense of purpose to appreciate the importance of this observation. Workers do use 'aesthetic' terms to identify good work; in the context of an argument which locates such reference to a general 'aesthetic' of social work it would become possible to outline procedures and terms which would facilitate the critical review of social work practice. If social work can really be 'beautiful' we can consider whether attempts to throw light on the nature of 'beauty' will also illuminate the nature of social work.

It is a measure of current confusion that it may seem absurd to take seriously an idea of 'beautiful social work'; it evokes a world altogether remote from the apparent experience of contemporary social work agencies and social work education. People do not look for beauty in the social services department, the probation office or the social work curriculum. Rapoport notes these apparent incongruities but is clear that the problem lies not in this conception of social work, which only reflects the experience of good social work, but in the pattern or organization, administration and education for social work. The problem persists; in the introduction to Rapoport's 'selected writings' (Katz, 1975), Carol Meyer refers to the difficulties of a quest for excellence in social work in a 'hostile' climate. Any view of social work, therefore, which elucidates an understanding of the social worker as artist may clarify the pervasive but elusive difficulties in seeking appropriate administration and education in social work.

These difficulties are currently well known, but they must inevitably persist until some means is found the better to grasp the nature and implications of subjectivity in social work.

Rapoport's account points to the way in which this subjectivity may be explored, but her limited concern with creativity did not lead her to reflect upon the related matters of knowledge, understanding and action in social work. She suggests the pervasive implications of her comments, but does not substantiate them with any developed exploration of art itself or of the institutions necessary for its maintenance. But she, together with those writers concerned to extend the sensitivity and sensibility of the social worker, gives considerable credence to the proposition that social work must necessarily be viewed as an artistic activity. These authors, including even Rapoport, do not define the field of inquiry; they are somehow still constrained by the obligations of social science. They do, however, by implication or assertion, make it very evident that it exists. The need then is to identify in more detail the ways in which the subjectivity of social work can be rendered accessible by an exploration of art theory, and to consider the practice implications if such access were to be established. These issues will be the themes of the next two chapters.

8

... but is it Art?

UNDERSTANDING: EXPLORING THE SHIFTING GROUND

Social work is an activity dependent primarily upon the process of understanding other people, and communication and activity based closely upon that understanding – a description in which understanding can now be given, after Rickman, the 'special meaning of sympathetic insight into the mental life of other people'. It is clear that such understanding is different from explanation, in'that it is not empirically verifiable; the perceived and the percipient are both ephemeral. How then are they to be grasped?

Elizabeth Irvine's (1974) paper on the links between social work and literature suggests the problem; she notes that the language of literature is imprecise, but considers that 'an ambiguous language reflects a fluid reality, which can be evoked and thus to some extent communicated, but cannot be pinned down or immobilized'. It may be the case that literature cannot be 'immobilized', but the scale of the operation of 'art appreciation' – institutions for education and study in the arts and for the propagation and criticism of the arts (and in some states for their control) – bears witness not only to their enormous power and importance, but to a belief in some form of intelligible discussion about them (a discussion to which Irvine herself of course contributes). Consider, by comparison, both the similarity and the difference from Irvine's account in this extract from Percy Lubbock's *The Craft of Fiction*:

> To grasp the shadowy and fantasmal form of a book, to hold it fast, to turn it over and survey it at leisure – that is the effort of the

critic of books, and it is perpetually defeated. Nothing, no power, will keep a book steady and motionless before us, so that we may have time to examine its shape and design. As quickly as we read, it melts and shifts in memory ... A cluster of impressions, some clear points emerging from the mist of uncertainty, that is all we can hope to possess, generally speaking, in the name of a book. (quoted in Gotshalk, 1962)

The critic or artist – it will become clear that the roles have significant common characteristics – therefore seeks to handle that same 'fluid reality' but he believes it will be both possible and worthwhile to grasp 'some clear points'. He recognizes its ephemerality but he seeks nonetheless to identify important perspectives towards his material; however, he does not seek to render an exhaustive account of it. This incomplete process of clarification is not understood to be a frustrated science; it is a distinct but intellectually dignified activity.

Social work has characteristics of both art and criticism. The social worker starts with some of the faculties of the critic; he tries to understand the communications of his clients, how they in turn understand, experience and give meaning to the world. He is trying, in F. R. Leavis's (1962) terms, 'to determine what is actually *there*'. T. S. Eliot (Kermode, 1975), writing of the 'perfect critic', concluded similarly that in criticism 'we aim to see the object as it really is'. This is not a process which can be done by any defined formula in social work, nor in art. Consider Leavis's (1962) comments on literature and philosophy:

[Literature demands] not merely a fuller bodied response, but a completer responsiveness – a kind of responsiveness which is incompatible with the judicial, one-eye-on-the-standard approach. The critic – the reader of poetry – is indeed concerned with evaluation, but to figure him as measuring with a norm which he brings up to the object and applies from the outside is to misrepresent the process. The critic's aim is, first, to realize as sensitively and completely as possible this or that which claims his attention ...

It is the realization of an experience, rather than the explanation of an idea.

Leavis's description identifies a familiar problem. The critic's concern with 'evaluation' can be paralleled by the social worker's foreknowledge that he must 'evaluate' his clients. This evaluation precedes any formal assessment he may prepare for court or agency; his own perception is itself an evaluation, built upon the various schemeta or constructs he uses to understand his clients. The social worker, like the critic, must ensure that his perception is widely based and thus as potentially flexible as possible; and in both fields a widely based knowledge is recognized as an important component of this flexibility: it helps achieve the understanding of meaning. In other words, the social worker can make more sense with more available perspectives. But Leavis's reference to 'the outside' is a measure of the limitations on such knowledge. The difference between philosophy and poetry, between science and art, is substantially that knowledge cannot be applied from 'outside'. Leavis's approach to poetry thus has much in common with the knowledge required for social work, and with the form of understanding defined by Rickman; the knowledge required cannot be precisely defined and its realization is partly a matter of personal sensibility.

Gotshalk's account of 'aesthetic experience' in *Art and the Social Order* (1962) confirms and clarifies this view. This early stage of the social work process might be likened to 'aesthetic' perception in art appreciation. In the aesthetic experience 'the great concern is to let all that is present in the object appear to the self in the fullest and most vivid manner'. It is similar to the disinterested respect, the empathic acceptance that social worker's prize in their professional attitudes to their clients. But Gotshalk is clear that such 'aesthetic' appreciation requires much more than intellectual effort.

> It would be no exaggeration to say that alert perception brings into action, in one form or another, the total being of the percipient ... In consequence, the sensory, intuitive, imaginative, emotional, and intellectual generators..., the telic and physiological factors; and the backgrounds of memory, knowledge, personality, and character are opened up ...

This is a comprehensive list, and a long way (apparently) from the approaches of a positivist science. But it is a list of characteristics which is required if an adequate distinction is to be made between explanation and understanding. Yet social work, like art, demands the 'realization of experience', for it is only by this diverse procedure that knowledge from the 'inside' can be acquired. Gotshalk's account looks familiar as the necessary equipment of the social worker. (Gotshalk in fact, in an incidental but relevant remark, suggests that in helping someone with a 'distressing personal problem' perception becomes too instrumental to be deemed aesthetic: the context of this remark, however (in which he likens perceptions in helping and taking a drink of milk in their instrumental quality), suggests that he has rather an unreal view of the helping process – nor is his remark consistent with his later emphasis upon the value of art in professional and social life.)

These critics place an emphasis upon subjective characteristics in perception, appreciation and understanding in art. That emphasis requires a consequent attention upon the self, the locus of that subjectivity; 'the tests of realization', writes Leavis (1962), 'are applied in the operation of the critic's sensibility; they are a matter of his sense, derived from his ... experience, of what the living thing feels like'. Such sensibility, Leavis makes clear elsewhere in the same work, is not universal; literature is 'accessible only to the reader capable of intelligent and sensitive criticism'. T. S. Eliot also sees acute perception as a distinct and distinguished ability, though he appears to place more emphasis upon the intellect: 'perceptions do not, in a really appreciative mind, accumulate as a mass, but form themselves as a structure' (Kermode, 1975); this he sees as the development of 'sensibility'. Wellek and Warren (1970), who developed a theory of literature they termed 'perspective realism', discuss the role that cultural values will play in perspectives in literature; the 'values exist potentially in the literary structures; they are realized, actually valued, only as they are contemplated by those who meet the requisite conditions [of capacity and training]'.

The relevance of these writings is that the authors seek to identify the means of getting access to a 'fluid reality', a 'shadowy and fantasmal form'. They assert that access *is* possible, but that it requires a full and adequate response from all the faculties of the percipient – not just the 'intellectual generators', but the sensory, intuitive, imaginative and emotional ones have to be deployed. They are aware that it is only by their combined use that man can ever experience and understand the world. Social workers are engaged in getting access to this same 'fluid reality' and their task requires a similar subjectivity; their work must therefore demand the possession of a similarly developed, distinct sensibility. The disciplined recognition and development of this sensibility is for social work, as for the artist and the critic, one of the major professional tasks to be mastered; social workers must possess such developed sensibility if they are to understand their client's worlds. To learn something of the nature of understanding, then, it is necessary – in Eliot's phrase – to consider how these perceptions form themselves into a sensible structure.

UNDERSTANDING: COHERENCE AND COMPLEXITY

The subject matter of social casework is the individual human being as he exists in reality, that is, in a total situation ... Casework does not deal with some particular segment of the individual, but with the individual as a whole person.

The problem of the 'whole man' in social work precedes Bowers's (1949) exploration, and has persisted through the subsequent shift in emphasis from 'casework' to a more balanced 'social work'. Whether alone, in families or in community groups the distinguishing concern of the social worker is his need to understand and extend the way people construct and interpret their effective world, and these constructions and interpretations are always unique. The perception and experience of the individual as a whole person, and of individuals as whole people, rest at the centre of social work. Social work must therefore always be aspiring to the infinite complexity of experience, and trying to render this complexity coherent. This is a problem familiar in art.

[The diversity of material] may mean particularly ideas, characters, types of social and psychological experience. Eliot's celebrated instance in 'The Metaphysical Poets' is relevant. By way of showing that the poet's mind is 'constantly amalgamating disparate experience', he imagines such a whole formed of the poet's falling in love, reading Spinoza, hearing the sound of a typewriter, and smelling something cooking ... Our principle here would be that, provided a real 'amalgamation' takes place, the value of the poem rises in direct ratio to the diversity of its materials. (Wellek and Warren, 1970)

This extract serves to do more than confirm that a synthesis of elements is an integral aspect of art; it gives some indication of a criterion by which this synthesis may be judged. For it is evident that some such synthesis of elements is an aspect of ordinary human perception. The poet's *distinct* perception is therefore a variation on common perception – in the same way that, as earlier discussion noted, the synthesized understanding of the social worker is similar in kind to common understanding. There is, however, no doubt that the poet does have a special perception, a special understanding, and it seems to be an intense form of common perception or understanding. The poet and social worker are both striving to realize a synthesis of diverse material. The criterion of the poet may then be an aid to the social worker – perhaps he too can look to the yardsticks of 'real amalgamation' and 'diversity'.

This clarifies the other analogous role of the social worker, artist as well as critic. His primary task may require of him the faculties of the critic, the aesthetic ability which helps him see with greater clarity the 'meaning' of his clients' communications. But he must also make sense of all his information, of which his client's communications will only be a part, by bringing it together in some form. This he does by forming a mental 'picture' of the material; this is his intuitive knowledge. It is not just that he must have his knowledge instantly available to inform his immediate behaviour with his clients; it is the nature of such diverse material that it can be brought together, in part at least, only by such intuitive means. The selection and synthesis must be a matter of individual consciousness, for the material available is potentially infinite. We can only possess the 'cluster of impressions that emerge from the mists of uncertainty', those points our subjective consicousness selects. There is no alternative to this procedure, for there is no way that all the available stimuli could be identified and evaluated, even with endless time. With time, though, the synthesis which forms the mental 'picture' can be analysed; it is the picture which is the starting point for any subsequent intellectual inquiry. The social worker, then, like the poet, must bring together disparate elements of the ordinary world, and he too must do so with unusually profound understanding, for his understanding must enrich the understanding of his clients. It is in this sense that the worker is creative; he is not just a critic understanding the meaning and expression of others, but an artist giving expression to his own understanding in a way that others will value.

The image of the 'picture' is an important one, for it suggests a visible completeness, sufficient to guide the worker's subsequent action. This is what seems to happen; the worker gets a sense of his client's meaning, and this sense guides him in his immediate behaviour – for the worker has, in most of his work, to act immediately, and the soundness of that behaviour will be the important determinant of his overall helpfulness. As there is no way of 'not responding' to distressed or angry clients, the worker must immediately make sense of his client's world; he must get an adequate picture of it. The nature of human experience means that the worker's picture, like an image in art, must be not merely 'a unification of disparate ideas' but 'that which presents an intellectual and emotional complex in an instant of time' (Ezra Pound, quoted in Wellek and Warren, 1970). Imagery in some guise is therefore routinely essential in social work, and it becomes clear why vivid images and evocative language are so frequent a characteristic of good descriptions of social work.

The image, the artist's work, must include not merely 'diversity' but 'real amalgamation'. The poet's reading of Spinoza must be effectively linked with the smell of cooking, the client's outburst of anger with the courage of his new approach to his problems. Diversity alone will be haphazard, a disorganized collection of fragments; it will have no meaning. A man must give meaning to events to give them sense; his picture must have not merely complexity but coherence. These are evidently qualities necessarily present in all perception, but in art they acquire an enhanced and interrelated intensity. Wellek and Warren make it clear that these values, coherence and complexity, are central to art. Gotshalk has a similar expression, 'an individuated diversity governed by integrity and harmony'. But to the social worker these are recognizable descriptions; they suggest the selection and synthesis, the coherence and complexity of social work assessments – as they must, for they too are enhanced forms of ordinary perception. Coherence and complexity must be criteria to be brought to any assessment of the social worker's intuitive knowledge. They are part of an approach to the subjectivity of social work.

Works of coherence and complexity cannot be constructed to formula, for while knowledge and experience, preparation and circumstance may help direct their shape, they are necessarily the expression of personal perception and personal meaning. Art, like criticism, therefore also requires personal qualities. Gotshalk has attempted to identify these qualities:

> The capacity to be keenly affected by the perceptual world, to gather 'facts', and to lay up memories convertible into a great symbolic repertory is usually called 'sensitivity'. The power to reintegrate this repertory, to construct from it images of novel perceptual systems, to shape 'the facts into the fabric of vision', is usually called 'imagination'.

Such personal qualities are, to an extent, amenable to educational change; we 'learn' to see and interpret the world, and we can therefore try to direct that learning. But they are, at root, attributes of being, of consciousness. Thus the ability to explore the shifting ground, to 'gather facts and to construct images', to select information and give it some adequate synthesis – in short, the ability to understand – requires distinct qualities of sensitivity and imagination. Not only are these the distinct faculties of the artist and the critic, they also offer to the artist and critic a framework for evaluation. The concepts of coherence and complexity may sound unfamiliar to the social worker, but they are relevant because the social worker aspires to that same understanding as the artist. They are also relevant because of their use for evaluation, for although social work has sought for evaluative criteria which have more apparent precision than 'coherence and complexity', it has sought in vain. If social work is to be seen as art, then such concepts may help social work construct a genuinely viable approach to the criticism and assessment of practice.

COMMUNICATING UNDERSTANDING

Social workers need what Eliot once called a 'sense of fact' if they are to get some access to the diversity of experience. This sense, according to Eliot in his essay on 'The function of criticism'

(Kermode, 1975), is the faculty which is important above all others to the 'practitioner critic', and the social worker, it is already clear, must master both roles as integral aspects of his own role. Armed with a sense of fact to penetrate the shifting ground, the social worker's 'picture' will reflect the complexity of the real world. He must then bring to this picture a sense of coherence to make it intelligible and purposeful. But, as the earlier analysis showed, the social worker must also have an aptitude for appropriate intuitive behaviour as well as this capacity for intuitive, subjective understanding, and this aptitude, whether the behaviour is discussion or activity, rests largely on the ability to communicate understanding accurately. The nature of this communication is the kernel of the analogy (or rather of the link, for the connection becomes more substantial than mere similarity) between social work and art.

The theoretical analysis from which this link is developed is put forward by Raymond Williams in an essay on 'The creative mind' in *The Long Revolution* (1965). This paper is rich in material which can contribute to an analysis of social work, but in particular, Williams asserts that communication is the essential element in art, and that the processes of communication and understanding are one. His analysis gives substance not only to the concept of 'intuitive behaviour' in social work, but an unexpected reaffirmation of the central importance of such communication by offering an intelligible way of giving more precise shape to the meaning of 'social' work – a difficult concept that has refused either to disappear or to become clear for social work theorists.

Williams writes to explore problems in the theory of culture, and problems of 'meaning and action'. He reports the difficulty of finding any single academic disciplined in which these questions can be examined: 'At one level we can oppose art to science, or emotion to reason, yet the activities described by these names are in fact deeply related parts of the whole human process.' He notes that his novel *Border Country* is part of the same personal body of work as *The Long Revolution* (and *Culture and Society*), in other words that, in this instance, the 'imaginative' and 'analytical' works are integral parts of the same whole. Williams has as his starting point a recognition of the constraints of abstract disciplines, constraints which are equally problematic for social work, and in his studies of culture he has not found the disciplinary divisions to be tenable.

It is Williams's thesis that each man has constantly to construct his own understanding of the world, and that this understanding can only be formulated by communication. Good art is a particularly skilled mastery of the ordinary means of communication, but it is nonetheless essentially these ordinary means of communication. The process of communication is the process of finding common meaning, and thus the process of finding community, and so society; art is therefore a measure of the social and psychological state of being. The princpal importance, for social work, of Williams's thesis is that he develops a concept of meaning of which communication is an integral part. The meaning must be communicated to be realized, and so he makes the 'communication of meaning' a necessary aspect of human well-being, and its finer accomplishment the aspiration of all art. This account is partially familiar to social work from other sources, notably the Rogerian and Laingian emphases upon the importance for mental health of empathic understanding, of not only recognizing the experience of others but communicating that recognition. It confirms the experience, especially common for social workers, of the relief and help which can come just from the process of communicating understanding, even without further action. But it also helps to root this ephemeral and subjective procedure – Williams makes it clear that this is the process which underlies all art.

The contemporary starting point for Williams's inquiry is the work of the biologist, J. Z. Young. He notes Young's claim that each person's brain 'literally' creates that person's own world. There is no necessary connection between the experience of the senses and the sense we make of experience:

> Contrary to what we might suppose, the eyes and brain do not simply record in a sort of photographic manner the pictures that pass in front of us ... Many of our affairs are conducted on the assumption that our sense organs provide us with an accurate record, independent of ourselves. What we are now beginning to realize is that much of this is an illusion, that we have to learn to see the world as we do. (J. Z. Young, *Doubt and Certainty in Science – A Biologist's Reflections on the Brain*, quoted in Williams, 1965)

Aaron Scharf, in *Introduction to Art* (Open University, 1971), gives examples of this process. Of particular interest are studies of subjects who, once blind, later acquire sight. Such studies make it clear that the 'meaning' of objects must be learned before they can be grasped; that for example, even after considerable learning, there may be difficulty in perceiving the difference between a sphere and a cube. (Scharf illustrates this process of learning with a report of a missionary who dropped photographs of himself from the air, hoping to lessen the possible threat of his subsequent arrival. 'Unfortunately, the natives could make no sense of the shadowy language of the pictures, and when the missionary arrived they ate him.') Scharf discusses experiments with animals, which seem to have less difficulty with such learning, and concludes that the need to learn to see may be the price that must be paid for the faculty of imagination.

This knowledge of perception leads Williams to conclude that there can be no reality into which man's observations and interpretations do not enter. This position is now partially familiar; the very different works of Abercrombie (1969; Abercrombie also acknowledges the influence of J. Z. Young), Berger and Luckmann (1967), and Kelly (1980), for example, have already been mentioned. But Williams first of all makes clear how fundamental is this process to material as well as to social perception. He notes Young's description of a 'cycle of organization', in which patterns of understanding of the world are created which then change, and continues:

> Since this continuing organization and reorganization of consciousness is, for man, the organization and reorganization of reality – the consciousness a way of learning to control his environment – it is clear that there is a real sense in which man can be called a creator.

Secondly, he makes clear that it is necessary to communicate in order to create this reality. It is necessary to describe reality in order to interpret it either by a known or newly developed configuration, for only by description can man know how to handle phenomena. There is always, therefore, a 'vital descriptive effort'. But description cannot be an ultimate activity:

> description is a function of communication ... [Experience] has to

be described to be realized (this description being, in fact, putting the experience into a communicable form) and has then, because this is the biological purpose of the description, to be shared with another organism.

It follows from this that:

> It is ... to everyman a matter of urgent personal importance to 'describe' his experience, because this is literally a remaking of himself, a creative change in his personal organization ... [The] impulse to communicate is a learned human response to disturbance of any kind. For the individual of course the struggle is to communicate successfully by describing adequately ... unless the description is adequate, there can be no relevant communication. To think merely of making contact with others, rather than of making contact with this precise experience, is irrelevant and distracting. Genuine communication depends on this absorbed attention to precise description, but of course it does not follow that the description is for its own sake; the attention rather is a condition of relevant communication.

Finally, Williams makes clear that 'communication' is a reciprocal term; mere expression is insufficient: 'any adequate description of experience must be more than simple transmission; it must also include reception and response'. Williams's argument has a profound significance for any approach to helping which recognizes the importance of shared understanding, of 'real' understanding of experience. Williams's account shows that people *make* their understanding of the world, that description through communication is an essential part of understanding, and that communication must be exact, and effectively shared. In the most fundamental way, each person's ability to make sense, and to organize an understanding of the world, depends upon the ability to communicate about that understanding. 'Reality' is only maintained by its communication, and such communication is particularly urgent at times of stress.

This account is immediately recognizable in a model of social work which gives weight to the therapeutic value of such principles as acceptance and respect for persons, and is particularly close to the client-centred model's concepts of confirmation and empathy. Indeed it is a commonplace that a 'problem shared' is a profound help at times of stress, and the client-centred helper's emphasis upon accurate empathy recognizes this. (It is not a commonplace that accurately empathic help, from friends or professionals, is actually available at times of stress; the confused criticism, 'they tried to be helpful, but they didn't understand' is frequent witness to this.) Williams's account is concerned with art, not with social work, but to social workers, and others (although for others it does not fulfil the central, essential role), it gives an added clarity to that process of the recognition of experience which is of such profound importance. It makes fundamental sense of the relief and gratitude people show in response to accurate understanding, for they have, literally, been helped to exist. The social worker has to communicate that understanding of the client's experience, and do so with detailed exactness; no less will do. This process is a fine and subtle affair, and it requires considerable power. In Williams's view the process of sharing understanding is the process of creativity in art – or rather, it is an ordinary process, but the artist has command of 'powerful means' of sharing. All people are artists in that all people must make and communicate meaning. The creative insight of the 'good' artist is shared with others who have the 'creative imagination' to find and organize new descriptions of experience.

The skill of the artist lies in his transmission; art is an intense form of 'ordinary' human communication. Such communication is a profoundly personal process, for it is an expression of the most intimate meaning. Because the 'objective' world is 'subjectively' created, its realization is a matter of constant personal creativity, of individual effort and individual perception:

> Since the meaning and the means cannot be separated, it is on the artist's actual ability to live the experience that successful communication depends. By living the experience we mean that . . . the artist has literally made it part of himself, so deeply that his whole energy is available to describe it and transmit it to others. Bad art is then the failure or relative failure of this kind of personal organization, which we know now to be more than a figure of speech but an actual process by which we live. Our actual human organization is for the purpose of communicating, and in art as in other kinds of communication . . . the ability to communicate is not a matter of abstract qualities, such as feeling, intelligence or will, but

is rooted in certain whole patterns of organization; success or failure is a matter of the whole self. (Williams, 1965)

Meaning and communication, then, are inextricably linked, and inextricably a function of 'the whole self'; they are rooted in 'whole patterns of organization'. Art consequently can be seen to be not only a matter of coherence and complexity, but of articulate and intimately personal communication, of experience that must be lived. Social work's essential emphasis upon intuitive behaviour, upon the communication of understanding, is thus as firmly placed in the theory of art as the preceding procedures of intuitive understanding, of selection and synthesis. Art recognizes and affirms social work's emphasis not only upon expression, but upon the necessarily intimate, personal character of that expression.

SOCIAL WORK IN THE TRADITION OF ART

It becomes clear that there are substantial grounds for locating social work within the tradition of art. Art offers recognition and exploration of the ephemerality which marks the subject matter of all social work; it knows the practices of selection and synthesis which social workers must undertake if their understanding is to be adequately complex and coherent; it places the same high value upon the communication of that understanding. Art strengthens social work's theory; it shows that the communication of understanding, which social workers know to be the key element in effective helping, is important in helping because it is important in living; it shows that such communication is the only route to understanding and so to personal sanity and social cohesion.

Such descriptions, however, pose at least as many problems as they solve. Most obviously, the discussion of theory in art has relied upon only a few works and ignored complexities and disagreements about the nature of art which are at least as wide as those about the social sciences. But it is not necessary to resolve these issues at this stage, for it is sufficient for the present discussion to note that the terms of a debate about art are relevant to a debate about social work. Given the relevance of these terms, it will follow that attempts to clarify the nature of social work as an art will be more fruitful than attempts based solely upon a scientific paradigm. An assessment of the nature of social work must necessarily include examination of social work as art as well as social work as science; both are clearly integral and essential parts of the whole. Without this duality, no inquiry into social work can have an adequate framework for analysis, nor can any analysis be complete. Analyses of social work within this framework will inevitably be just as problematic and contentious as the theory and criticism of art in general. But these problems and contentions will indicate the direction of the best accessible clarity for social work, of an intelligible reality or truth which must be realized as a condition of social work's ability to use any fragmented 'scientific' reality. It is, in all manner of meanings, the only way in which social work can make sense.

One necessary sense that social work must acquire will be evidently more intelligible within this tradition, for social work in its confusion and distress entirely fails to fulfil the wider social role for which it is distinctly qualified. To identify social work as art in this way is to assert essential social values, for the individual, and the individual as a whole person, lies at the root of art, most intelligibly in literature. This helps maintain, wrote Leavis (1962), 'the truth that human life lives only in individuals; I might have said, the truth that it is only in individuals that society lives'. Yet with the passing of the common importance of the church there is no institution which seeks to clarify the personal or moral meaning of social issues and events; social work, like art, should be one of the means by which we try to promote such learning, for it evidently belongs not in the sphere of health and treatment to which it has sometimes been assigned, but in the sphere of education.

It is also clear that social work cannot be confined as a 'clinical' activity. The old (perhaps always unreal) stereotype of casework with its focus solely upon the individual is evidently untenable. Raymond Williams (1965) in a discussion of realism in the novel, comes close to the proper emphasis of social work: 'In the highest realism society is seen in fundamentally personal terms, and persons, through relationships, in fundamentally social terms.' In his view, novels which examine only personal relationships, without an adequate social context, exhibit 'a failure of

consciousness, a failure to realize the extent to which the substance of a general way of life actively affects the closest personal
experience'. In the best realistic literature we attend carefully,
'with our whole senses', to this general life, 'yet the centre of value
is always the individual human person – not any one isolated
person, but the many persons'. Thus the plausible strength of
good social work and literature is that they examine the interaction of the general way of life and the closest personal experience. Williams asserts that there is, significantly, no contemporary tradition of the realist novel. It is a measure of the potential
importance of social work to our general culture that it is one of
the few institutions that could identify and further in general life
that integration which he believes is so central a value.

The key to this importance is implied by a phrase in an earlier
quotation, that 'our actual human organization is for the purpose
of communicating'. Williams had argued that reality is established and maintained only by communication, and our energy
must therefore be directed towards that communication. By
communicating we are able to make sense of our own experience,
and to make it common; we must similarly share the unique
experience of others. The ability to articulate meaning is the
ability to share meanings, and thus to offer the basis of social life
and social development, of negotiating cultural growth and
change. Human community 'grows by the discovery of common
meanings and common means of communication'. The artists'
role is to be skilled in helping others experience meanings –
familiar and innovatory. Both must be constantly asserted, to
maintain cohesion and to adapt to change, and both make
demands simultaneously upon the social and the personal organization.

It is therefore of immense importance for social and individual
well-being to ensure that a society is able to articulate and
negotiate the most subtle expressions of the meaning of experience, at all levels. The 'fatally wrong approach', asserts Williams,
is the assumption that different areas of life are separate, that
politics and art, and science and religion, for example, are
absolute categories. 'Every kind of activity in fact suffers, if it is
wholly abstracted and separated.' It is necessary first to have
some sense of the whole texture, and then to divide into instrumental abstractions. A sense of art can clearly offer a measure of

the whole texture, and with a sense of art many of the major social institutions could acquire the rounded ability to integrate and handle meaning, to recognize experience; art would no longer be 'excluded from serious practical concerns' as, Williams notes, it has recently been in our society.

Social work thus manifestly belongs in the tradition of art, and it has a considerable potential value as a social institution practised in striving for the 'whole texture'. In a strictly practical way, it can offer not only help in negotiating new meanings with those undergoing stress and change, but an example of the routine reality and importance of 'making sense' of the experienced world of other people. It is a need fundamental to all the personal services in health, education and welfare, and relevant to infinitely larger aspects of our organizational and institutional life. Social work is not, it has been shown repeatedly, a skill or understanding which can ever be exclusive to social workers. But social work could, if it could but see the way, offer to a society in need a model of the way in which such understanding and skill can be learned and used. Social work will never have a monopoly, but it will always have a special concentration of ability because it, alone amongst the helping professions, depends centrally upon such understanding and communication. In any modern society in which a creative and humane attitude was profoundly established, social work should have a significant role; conversely, social work has within its grasp the potential to further significantly the development of just such a genuinely civilized society.

9

Good Practice for Social Work

SOCIAL WORK AND CRITICISM

It is the evident weakness of social work that it has not found any adequate critical apparatus with which to evaluate its practice. The absence of a 'technical' measure, like the apparent yardsticks of health or learning in other fields, has confounded public and profession alike and compounded social work's crisis of confidence and plausibility. Evaluations of social work practice have failed to satisfy critics that a properly defined process and product has been identified, so social workers fear either that their work has no effect or that its effect is unmeasurable. As a result, social work has no system for the evaluation of practice competence, agencies have no developed procedure for examining the practice of their workers and, according to the research of Brandon and Davies (1979), even qualifying social work courses do not actually assess practice competence. Yet it goes against the dictates of experience and common sense, as well as the logic of professional qualification, to assert that all people are uniformly helpful; social workers *know* that social work can be done well and badly, but they cannot articulate this knowledge. Social work must find means to recognize and evaluate good practice.

The location of social work in the tradition of art gives social work access to the critical traditions of art. The evaluation of good and bad art is a difficult and contentious process, but it is an accepted process; by some means a consensus is reached sufficient to render plausible, for example, the operation of museums and libraries for the arts, and education and assessment in the study of the arts. These institutions show the possibility of adopting a critical approach to intuitive understanding and communication from which social work must learn.

Criticism in social work, as in art, is integral to practice, and social work practice requires not only the faculties of the artist but those of the critic. The social worker is critic in two distinct respects. Initially he is the critic of his client. This role, already outlined above, is clearer now in the light of Williams's designation of the meaning and communication of all people as a kind of art. All people are therefore both 'creators' (as communicators of meaning) and, by implication, 'evaluators' (as recipients of those communications). Artists have a particularly skilled mastery of these means of communication and, by implication, critics a particularly skilled mastery of the means of evaluation. The social worker has to be particularly skilled at the evaluation, or understanding, of his client's meaning and is thus his client's critic. But the worker's subsequent behaviour and communication is his 'art', and as this must necessarily be evaluated (to ensure that it serves the best interests of his client), the worker is also critic in the more profound sense that he must evaluate this 'art'. This process will not, of course, be always a dominantly conscious one, but its achievement will rest upon the worker's acquisition of practised critical sensibilities; the worker must possess developed critical powers if he is to be an effective critic. Criticism then, for both these reasons, is an integral though unrecognized element in the practice of social work. Its proper development will lead directly to the improvement of the general standard of practice. It will also serve a wider end, for the development of an adequate criticism will make social work 'visible' and will thus allow for its much broader understanding. It will be the means to a real exploration and analysis of social work.

THE NATURE OF CRITICISM

It is the purpose of artistic criticism, and art, to realize subjectivity, not to deny it. This process is not to abandon judgement but rather to judge, strenuously and detachedly, the nature of our own diverse experience. The critic tries to determine quality in the form, the coherence and complexity, and the communication of art. This process, the comments of different critics makes very clear, demands real evaluation to avoid an anarchic state – a state that is already familiar to social workers. Welleck and Warren, for example, in *Theory of Literature* (1970), refer to the dangers of that same 'anything goes' approach which has already been identified in social work: 'In its extreme formulation the anti-scientific solution has ... obvious dangers. Personal "intuitions" may lead to a merely emotional "appreciation", to complete subjectivity.' Eliot, in 'The function of criticism' (Kermode, 1975), writes of 'the inner voice' which is sometimes thought to determine an attitude to art: 'The inner voice, in fact, sounds remarkably like an old principle which has been formulated in the familiar phrase "doing as one likes".' He continues: 'The question is, the first question, *not* what comes natural or what comes easy to us, but what is right? Either one attitude is better than [another] ... or else it is indifferent. But how can such a choice be indifferent?' Leavis (1962) has a similar view, which he puts more starkly: 'the possibility of impersonality [is] ... implied in the existence of art'. In social work no less than art choices can never be indifferent, and yet they too are suspect because of their evident subjectivity. How then does the critic, and the practitioner who must be critic too, aspire to this impersonality? How do we identify good work?

Eliot's description of 'sensibility' shows that the process is similar to artistic creativity itself: 'Perceptions do not, in a really appreciative mind, accumulate as a mass, but form themselves as a structure; and criticism is the statement in language of this structure; it is a development of sensibility' (Kermode, 1975). We know in fact that it is not only in 'really appreciative minds' that perceptions form themselves into a structure, but the importance of this reference is the emphasis Eliot places upon the 'pattern' which forms in the critic's consciousness: perception and pattern, 'meaning', are once again the starting point for analysis. Leavis makes a similar assertion in relation to the critic's understanding of a new work of poetry:

> The organization into which it settles as a constituent in becoming 'placed' is an organization of similarly 'placed' things that have found their bearings with regard to one another, and not a theoretical system or a system determined by abstract considerations.

Criticism, then, is evidently itself a creative process. Indeed, it will become clear that good criticism must itself be a manner of artistic expression (albeit with a strictly defined focus) and must itself be judged partly by the canons of criticism.

The critic must use meaning, he must seek to establish, articulate and extend his immediate understanding and his intuitive consciousness. It is, in a more genuinely catholic and thorough sense than the traditional analytic casework use implied, a process of 'self-awareness'. Kermode identified three stages in Eliot's description of criticism; first, a surrender to an experience 'later to be integrated with a larger whole'; then a moment of recovery while the object of attention 'settles into the mind'; and thirdly, 'having something to say [which] requires speculation and systematization, perhaps historical and perhaps theoretical – faithful to the experience but providing it with an intellectual vehicle' (Kermode, 1975). Kermode writes that this process of creation and criticism, in Eliot's view, required considerable emotional and intellectual effort:

> The first moment, then, is one of emotional rather than intellectual engagement, and here the critic resembles the poet. He is not thinking: like the poet 'he starts from his own emotions' ... Later there comes the necessity of 'great intellectual power', necessary to the expression of 'precise emotion'. Just so the critic, most of all in the third phase of the operation, stands in need of intellect. This is what Eliot meant by saying that 'the only method is to be very intelligent'. The critic starts from his own emotions, but 'having something to say' calls for intellect. (Kermode, 1975)

Eliot's description is important because it fuses thought and feeling in a significant way. Eliot viewed the articulation of 'precise emotion' as a matter of intellect and, as this articulation is an important aspect of practice and criticism in social work, it points to the way in which the 'only method' in social work will require the worker 'to be very intelligent'. But it is also important because Eliot is outlining discrete stages which, in a social work context, will determine the way in which theory is used. The first stage constitutes 'experience', to be engaged in the event (as practitioner or critic); the second can be called 'picture' – the experience (presumably partly simultaneously) assumes a mental shape which is accessible to detection and description; and the third is 'analysis', in which we 'have something to say'. These stages outline the shape of the link between theory and practice in social work. 'Analysis' in social work must depend upon 'picture' which must depend upon 'experience'; analysis is not free from the requirement of fluency and intellectual rigour, but its basis in any specific instance must always be the picture which is derived from intuitive consciousness. The social worker (and the artist and the critic) can strive to ensure that his consciousness is informed by broad theoretical sensitivities and that his analysis makes full use of his abstract and intellectual grasp, but at the moment of 'experience' his ability to create a 'picture' is not a matter open to his full conscious control. Thus the analysis is in some sense bounded by the scope of the picture; there is inevitably some interaction, but this essentially personal constraint limits all analyses in social work, including formal and nominally 'objective' reports.

It is in this sense that all real analyses of social work are partially works of criticism and must be understood as such if they are themselves to be properly evaluated. The critic must have an 'experience' before he can have any relevant knowledge, and it is through this experience that he brings to bear his analytic powers, his application of the canons of coherence and complexity, and of effective communication. In all such evaluation, experience precedes analysis because analytic access is gained only through experience.

But analysis, and its necessary preliminaries, are only one half of criticism; the other is dialogue. Critical analysis must be accompanied by critical communication. Leavis made it clear that in his role as a critic he strove to make conscious, coherent and articulate his response so that he could help others to elucidate their own response, and to see that 'the essential order ... did, when they interrogated their experience, look like that to them also' (1962). It is this process of dialogue which, in Eliot's view as well, complements analysis:

> it occasionally happens that one person obtains an understanding of another, or a creative writer, which he can partially communicate, and which we feel to be fine and illuminating. It is difficult to confirm the 'interpretation' by external evidence. [Who] is to prove his own skill? ... [For] every success ... there are thousands of impostures. Instead of insight, you get fiction. Your test is to apply it again and again to the original, with your view of the original to guide you ... It is fairly certain that 'interpretation' ...

is only legitimate when it is not interpretation at all, but merely putting the reader in possession of facts which he would otherwise have missed ... Comparison and analysis ... are the chief tools of the critic. (Kermode, 1974)

Eliot, it can be noted, offers confirmation of the similarity between 'understanding another' and understanding the work of a creative artist. But the importance of the passage is that Eliot shows his solution to the problem of 'proof' to lie not only in repeated searching of consciousness (which can yield insights so clear that they can be called 'facts') but, as did Leavis, in appeal to the reader's own experience of the *same* art. Elsewhere Eliot writes of 'co-operative activity'; Leavis uses such phrases as 'social collaboration', 'a responsive community of minds' and 'a community of consciousness'. Comparison is thus essential, which means that critics must have access both to common creative expressions and to common critical accounts. Criticism in social work will therefore require the means to gain access both to common creative and critical accounts of practice.

One benefit of such critical practice will be the creation of a 'community of consciousness' within social work itself, for social work suffers directly from its present lack of any common professional culture. It follows from Williams's (1965) essay on the creative mind that the critic, like the artist, like everyone, is striving not only to identify but to share his meaning, for a function of this sharing is to create; the meaning of the critic too can only be realized in communication. But communication is only one element of Williams's broader concern, which is an examination of culture. Williams sees the process of communication, of establishing common meaning, as the process of creating community. This common meaning gives to 'culture' both its artistic and its anthropological significance, for it is the expression and fabric of social cohesion and coherence. Social work is in sore need of just such cohesion and coherence, of the creation of 'professional' community which can offer sanction and support. One gain, therefore, from the establishment of a framework for critical comparison within social work would be the necessary strengthening of a social work culture, and the eventual realization of a robust and substantial common identity in social work.

The greatest gain from the practice of an adequate criticism in social work, however, and the legitimating basis for any professional culture, would be the achievement of some clearer standard, some viable measure, to be used in professional practice. Such a measure in fact flows from the process of creating real community. Shared meanings are clearly relative and based upon value; indeed social reality requires such constant affirmation and confirmation precisely because it *is* based upon value. 'Comparison' therefore becomes the only way of aspiring towards any degree of objectivity in the assessment of perception. Abercrombie (1969) noted, in her discussions of the nature of human judgement, that 'there is no check for ... schemata other than talking about them, and thus comparing and contrasting them with other people's'. Critical exchange can be understood as an aspect of such a process, a process of affirmation and confirmation, comparison and contrast. The possible validity of art is established by a process of experience, then analysis, and then, through discussion and comparison of that analysis, by the achievement of some sufficiently shared understanding. In other words a state is achieved which is no longer only personal. Individual values are inherent in criticism but, by discussion, they become the values of the culture.

In the arts, dependence upon values is thus inevitably central, and seen to be so. Leavis (1962) wrote that in literature 'terms of value judgement figure essentially', and Wellek and Warren (1970) wrote that 'there is no structure outside norms and values. We cannot comprehend and analyse any work of art without reference to value.' It is only by the assertion of value that perception can select and synthesize, that it can bring manageable coherence to complexity. This means therefore that values are no base currency, but integral and fundamental to the whole, to be necessarily included in any analysis and discussion. In Welleck and Warren's *Theory of Literature* (1970) this emphasis is basic; they develop a critical approach based upon value which they call 'perspectivism' and which they describe as 'a process of getting to know the object from different points of view which may be defined and criticized in their turn'. Gotshalk (1962) writes similarly:

> To deny the temperamental colourings in works of art is not possible ... Under such circumstances the best plan for criticism

would seem to be to illumine these temperamental colourings in such a way that their value to diverse percipients is immediately clear or can be discovered and known with greater clarity. And this should be the aim of art criticism.

It should be the aim no less of criticism in social work. Social work's 'reality' is also subjective and value-laden, but this is not an impediment to evaluation; rather, it determines its particular nature and procedures.

Good social work rests upon the process of criticism, a process of experience and understanding, of analysis and comparison. A critical faculty is integral to the very practice of social work, to enable the worker to evaluate his client's and his own communications. A widespread and detailed critical dialogue is the only means whereby any canons of professional judgement and evaluation can be established in social work, through the establishment of common professional meanings and a common professional culture. This criticism, like art, and like life, is subjective, but it is the apparent fallacy of social work to assume that this precludes the possibility of inquiry, intellectual precision and impersonality. The opposite is true, for through criticism we may achieve some certainty about the real, experienced world. Indeed, through criticism, wrote Eliot (Kermode, 1975), there is the 'possibility of arriving at something outside ourselves, which may provisionally be called truth'.

CRITICAL PRACTICE IN SOCIAL WORK

Social work is like art and like criticism. It is insufficient to note only that social work is 'art-like', for it is also necessary to explore something of the nature of criticism in the arts to learn about the nature of social work itself, since social work is simultaneously both an artistic and a critical activity. The discussion of art and criticism makes possible a more rounded consideration of social work, and allows a grasp to be gained of the steps the social worker takes in integrating his learned theory and in integrating theory with practice. The discussion offers the route to a legitimate 'practice theory' for social work, and consequently a means of identifying and evaluating good practice. No framework or categorization of intuition can ever be complete, but the identification of social work as art does make possible the identification of discernible stages in 'critical practice'.

The social work process is a cycle of criticism, artistic creativity and criticism. In the first state the worker is a critic, to appraise the meaning of his client, whose communications may not be art (the client is unlikely to be master of an 'intense' form of communication) but will be 'art-like'. The worker deploys the steps of criticism – experience, analysis and comparison – to understand his client. He conducts this critical appraisal part consciously, part intuitively, implicitly comparing his analysis with the client to confirm his understanding. This is the first stage of the social work process.

The worker then becomes more originally creative. He articulates the meaning which the client's situation has for him as a worker, including as one element the client's own perception, and he communicates this understanding in a way which extends the client's own understanding. This communication may be in words or in action, fragmentary or extensive, but it will be a 'lived' communication, an expression of the worker's experience – his feelings, memories, associations, as well as his thoughts – expressed with immediacy and conviction. This is the worker's 'art'. His understanding and his communication must have the intensity to offer effective new meanings to his client. His art must be judged by the criteria of its complexity and coherence, and by the exactness of its communication.

But the worker must usually be the critic of his own art. His art is largely immediate, and therefore he must himself evaluate the effectiveness of his work with the client. He experiences and analyses his own behaviour, and conducts a form of comparison by explicit or implicit inquiry of his client. He *must* evaluate, for his behaviour must, in the interests of his client's welfare, be purposeful, and he will if necessary change his behaviour to fulfil this welfare need.

It is at this stage that social work, and the individual social worker, is evidently disadvantaged. This last critical stage marks the point at which the most thorough critical analysis is required, yet the worker must both act immediately, without the time for adequate analysis of his experience, and alone, without the chance for informed and extensive comparison. These constraints are inherent in social work, and they cannot be altered. Yet despite this immense demand upon the critical sensibilities of the worker, social work at present, whether in its agencies of practice, research or education, offers him almost no opportunity to assess his own critical ability. The social worker cannot know the value of his own evaluation, even though his evaluation underpins his entire practice.

This is not a necessary state of affairs. Indeed, it is evidently necessary that it be changed, for the worker must acquire a perspective upon his own critical judgement. But the development of a 'critical framework' is also necessary for more general reasons. The comparison of critical analyses of social work by social workers will mean communication within the profession of the 'meaning' which social workers give to their work. This process constitutes the only way to any adequate coherence for social work, the only way which may refute the suggestion that 'anything goes' and resolve the perennial vacuum that is evident whenever social workers seek to describe their role. 'Culture is the sharing of common meanings, and thence common activities and purposes; the offering, reception and comparison of new meanings, leading to the tensions and achievements of growth and change' (Williams, 1965). The current absence of a critical dialogue in social work means that there is no sharing of common meanings, and thus no sufficiently common activities and purposes, no coherent growth and change. There is no adequate social work culture.

The achievement of such critical dialogue in social work can only be achieved by the creation of public 'accounts' of social work, and then public criticism of those accounts – the equivalent, as it were, of art and critical debate about art. This is not the style of current critical writing in social work; there exists little in social work literature by way of creative accounts of practice, and less still by way of comparative or critical dialogue about such accounts. There is, in this sense, *no* contemporary critical literature in social work. Its 'analytic' writing is abstract and theoretical, whereas 'criticism should keep as close to the concrete as possible' (Leavis, 1962).

It is difficult to get access to full accounts of social work practice. Creative accounts, like the practice itself, are necessarily diverse, for they must simultaneously be evocations of the worker's experience – of the client's world and the worker in relation to the client's world – and analyses of the worker's perception and experience. No account of social work can divest itself of the two elements of creativity and criticism, of art and analysis. But existing accounts of social work usually seek to emphasize one element only, the critical element, thus trying to establish a division which is inherently impossible. This emphasis is most clearly evidenced in the common misperception about the status of formal reports in social work, for example, reports for the courts. Workers commonly perceive these as the fullest accounts of social work, as social work at its most detached and objective, reflecting the most significant judgements that they must make. Yet this perception, while it has some necessary plausibility, can quickly be shown to be a serious over-simplification.

Reports, like all social work analyses, are part of the stage of 'having something to say' which follows the stages of 'experience' and 'settling in the mind', the sequence which is characterized as experience, picture and analysis. Thus formal reports in social work are necessarily incomplete, because they give (usually) little account of the experience and picture from which they are derived. Such reports may have a structure and content which is appropriate enough for their purpose – for the lay readership in the court, for example – but they are in essence 'extracts' from more comprehensive critical accounts. Their weakness is that, in social work practice, these more comprehensive accounts are rarely written: social workers cite these formal reports as *the* analysis, and are unaware that no proper analysis exists. Writing such reports perhaps offers the opportunity for useful reflection, but such reflection is only sound if it is properly rooted (in adequate experience, in an adequate picture) and informed by adequate critical ability. Formal reports are not accounts of social work, yet they will usually be the fullest available accounts of practice. Indeed, despite the fact that they are usually written for 'laymen', they are often the basis for subsequent professional assessments and even for professional research.

This dearth of true accounts of social work in professional records reflects – presumably as both cause and effect – a similar lack of any rounded and creative emphasis in the few published accounts of social work. There are a few works which give an indication of the possible form of creative accounts of social work. An article by Ford and Hollick (1979), for example, seeks not only to narrate and evaluate the worker's consciousness, but to compare the contemporary view of the worker's client, and so merits attention both for its content and for its interesting narrative (joint narrative) form. An excellent book by Bill Jordan, *Helping in Social Work* (1979), sets out his experience as a worker, making it abundantly clear that thought and feeling, the personal and the impersonal, are all intimately part of the professional consciousness of the worker. Again, the form as well as the content of the book is of interest, for it is a mêlée of discussion with narrative and flashbacks, reminiscent in some ways of a novel by the same John Berger for whose work Jordan's appreciation has already been noted. Picardie's (1980) article, on an existential approach to social work, is similarly of interest in form as well as substance, for he not only discusses theoretical work, but also gives vivid, challenging and evocative accounts of practice which must, if he is to realize his theoretical end, achieve the imaginative engagement of his reader. Equally evocative, though very different in style, is Parsloe's (1972) narrative of her work with a probation client, recalling fluently the associations and perceptions which influenced her approach. These works offer examples of personally expressive and, to a degree, critical writing in social work. There are others, but only few others. Such works stand out distinctly in content and form, and show the possibility of a style of inquiry which must necessarily be added to social work's literature. But they do not yet constitute an established body of work.

This paucity of creative accounts severely limits the scope in social work for any critical dialogue. It does not preclude the possibility in agencies of routine commentary upon shared work, of the discussion of tape recordings or even of verbal reports (all of which must come to have a place in the critical repertoire), but it seems unlikely, with some exceptions in basic professional education, that many social workers do in fact engage in such discussion. Indeed, it would be surprising if they did so, for they have no common language or framework with which to maintain such discussion or to justify such inevitably personal comment. The professional culture does not legitimate or facilitate such entirely essential behaviour. This essential and personal critical practice can only be developed in a proper context. It needs a professional context of critical dialogue, of accessible critical activity and discussion. In other words, it needs a critical literature. 'Comparison' was Eliot's term, emphasizing the existence of not just one but a number of analyses. An *adequate* assessment of a single creative account requires not only that critics criticize, but that they review and compare the criticism of others – that they not only experience and analyse, but that they compare articulated experiences and analyses. The achievement of adequate critical practice in social work will thus require the publication of diverse critical analyses in response to specific published creative accounts of practice. Indeed, it is not an inappropriate fantasy, although perhaps far fetched, to envisage the publication of volumes of critical essays around celebrated pieces of good social work. It is certainly in this direction that social work should seek to travel.

Such developments would require a literary skill beyond the scope of most social workers. But it does not matter if the quality of good accounts and criticism is beyond the creative scope of the majority of us. What matters is that they exist and are accessible as a guide to the necessary efforts and judgements of every worker. It is in this way that the worker can become familiar with experience in social work, and able to analyse and compare its coherence, complexity and communication, and it is this process which gives him the basis for some defined critical competence. But this process of critical comparison also has a broader purpose, to offer social work access to common understanding about the experience and quality of practice, and so eventually to offer access to a coherent professional culture. Criticism thus offers scope for an understanding of the client, the worker and of social work itself; only by the development of 'critical practice', and all the stages it entails, can social work ever 'grow and change' and come to realize its real social value.

EDUCATION AND ORGANIZATION FOR GOOD PRACTICE

Social work as art and criticism legitimates sometimes contentious terms for inclusion in the professional vocabulary, terms such as intuition, human nature, and meaning. But if these terms are contentious, they are not unfamiliar; social workers have known of their professional relevance but not found the framework which would make them publicly plausible. Many of the characteristics of a genuinely relevant education and organization for social work are equally familiar, although they too have been obscured by confusion and contention.

The influence of good practice, critical practice, in social work must be pervasive. It must be evident in selection and curriculum in professional education, and in the workload, management, support, even working conditions of agency practice. There must, for example, be a properly searching and unashamed emphasis upon individual experience and individual perception in selection for social work, and an associated recognition of social work as an activity which requires a personal wisdom and maturity which is relatively rare, and can be increased but not created. There must, for example, be a recognition in social work education that the quest to identify a complete curriculum is inevitably frustrated; it is difficult because it is impossible, for social workers are neither masters nor slaves of any 'science', but necessarily and legitimately select their insights from catholic sources. There must, for example, be a recognition in social work agencies that social workers are only properly deployed where they focus upon the understanding and coping capacity of their clients, for although it may be the task of social service agencies to offer material services or advice these are not, in themselves, *social work* services and should be distinguished from them. There must, for example, be provision for social work practice which acknowledges the pivotal role of real understanding and communication, and makes provision for it – and, amongst other things, recognizes that this requires adequate interview facilities, for it cannot be easy to offer rich relationships in bare and thinly partitioned cupboards.

This list is extracted from a long and familiar litany, one which casts real doubt upon aspects of the current educational and organizational frameworks in social work. Social work exists in a 'hostile climate', not only because of its lay critics but because of the failure of its own institutions to create an adequate milieu, a failure rooted in social work's own incomprehension of its own nature. The complaints about insensitive structures of management and bureaucracy and about insensitive education are often justified, but social workers have lacked the ammunition and the clarity to articulate properly their objections to these insensitivities. The key to this confusion lies in the real recognition of the place of intuition and 'the person' in social work, and this present account will have had value if, in any degree, it increases the likelihood of their proper recognition.

The very familiarity of the litany does indicate that the principal elements of an appropriate education and organization for social work are already established, and that they need, not introduction, but an adequate priority which can be derived from a proper understanding of social work itself. Three areas merit specific comment in the context of this present discussion of social work as intuition, art and criticism: teaching social workers about the nature of their own professional knowledge; the place of the arts in social work education and practice; and most importantly, the need for a constant attention to the understanding and expressive ability of the individual social worker.

Social workers cannot have a defined body of knowledge and an exclusive expertise, and much of social work's practice knowledge is necessarily mediated through intuition. It is clear that, in a society which *nominally* seeks scientific credentials, this has been very much to social work's disadvantage. It is also clear though that this *need* not be perceived as a loss, since social value is also necessarily placed upon imagination and understanding, and the consequent task for social work is one of re-definition within these terms. Social workers need to be aware of the status of their professional knowledge, both to realize that it *is* proper knowledge, and to grasp the intellectual discipline which underpins such knowledge. Social work education curricula must therefore include some manner of epistemological studies, for social workers cannot be adequately equipped unless they have grasped why scientific credentials are both impossible and inappropriate for their task. The essential curriculum must also include two other linked but less philosophical elements: one, the study of the nature of human perception, the ways in which man imposes or creates meaning and its link with his ability to cope; the other, the aesthetic theory by which the expressions of such meanings may be subject to some measure of judgement. These elements together will constitute a genuine and distinct theoretical base for social work, necessary even if not sufficient. They will also make clear to the worker why the balance of his knowledge is neither defined nor distinct, why he necessarily extracts insights from a range of sources and why his knowledge at root is in fact his common sense.

It is likely that this curriculum will include material from the arts, but such studies will not be central; social work is art-like, but its study is not the study of the arts, rather it is *like* the study of the arts. But the use of art to increase understanding and sensitivity in the way described (see above, Chapter 7) is certainly to be encouraged. Such use should permeate the curriculum rather than be isolated within it, and it should be linked with systematic procedures allowing people to analyse and compare their perception of such material. This material, perhaps, is likely to be literature or narrative writing, though there is no reason why it should be exclusively so. Narrative, as Whan (1979) has noted, is of particular importance to social work. It is a form of expression which is 'democratic' in the sense that it is neither expert nor mysterious, and it allows for the dimensions of time and sequence which abstract accounts obscure. Indeed, 'the chief characteristic of narrative is its inclusiveness' (Welleck and Warren, 1970), and inclusiveness is certainly one characteristic (or failing) which has been attributed to social work. Narrative is the medium which best conveys elaborated or composite 'meaning', an extended common sense, and thus the social work curriculum could well place particular emphasis upon the 'narrataive studies', upon the novel, biography, drama and historical works. Such study though is not the principal outcome of the recognition of social work as art. It becomes an option but it is not the essential logic of such recognition.

It is important anyway that the social workers' use of art should not be limited to the 'consumption' of existing art; equally significant is the need for social workers and students to *be* artists. Social work must explore the scope of creative composition, in various forms, as a means of helping workers increase their powers of perception and expression, for if social work rests upon the worker's art, his ability to articulate his own meanings, then to require him to be 'artist' may be the best and most concise route to the identification and enhancement of these skills. This expressive use links in turn to the therapeutic potential of the arts, for by this rationale such creativity must be of use to clients at least as much as to workers; indeed, such use must clearly be of exceptional relevance to those in need of social work help, because of the role of art as a vehicle for social learning and cohesion. Yet the therapeutic use of art is a field which social workers have largely neglected; there are examples (e.g. see Rayner, 1977; Valk, 1979b) but they are rare. This field is one to which social workers will make greater reference and to which they should come to make distinct and significant contributions.

Above all else, though, good practice demands a general, constant and exact attention to the worker's understanding and expressive ability. It should not be an option but a necessity that both education and organization for social work give close and specific attention to the experience of the worker, to his 'person', yet it seems to be an option which in both fields is increasingly ignored. Social work's emphasis upon intuitive knowledge and intuitive behaviour, upon perception, meaning, expression and judgement, make central to social work the person and personality of the worker. This is the core of social work, whatever its setting or its scale; it is this core alone which distinguishes social work. There can be no social work without this emphasis upon the person and it is this emphasis which defines the distinct conditions which are conducive to good social work.

Good social work requires an intellectual, imaginative and emotional engagement which is intimate and precise, and is highly taxing of the person. It demands the identification and then the maintenance of distinct personal qualities. Professional education and organization must be structured primarily around these demands, and emphasize the procedures which will help to meet them, for it is these demands which are the very centre of professional practice and which determine the shape of all subsidiary knowledge and skill. Social workers must, as a matter of routine, take time with others to maintain and evaluate their own understanding and their own expression. These tasks are the essential basis of good practice and they must be continuing demands, a permanent feature throughout professional life. The social worker is only of value to his client if he has available adequate understanding and immediate responsiveness, and the worker *must* know of his current ability to meet these conditions. These attributes cannot be simply created (which is why social work requires a personal maturity which many people already know to be in short supply), but even after their identification they have to be sustained and extended. To do so takes time and resources.

The procedures to sustain and extend such resources are substantially familiar, but can now be recast in an unfamiliar light. The task for social workers and for social work students, above all else, is to assess and to extend their ability as both artist and critic. Their role as artist requires them to be astute about their own experience, perception and understanding and to be fluent in their expression, as well as to subject their ability to the critical scrutiny of others. Their role as critic requires them to evaluate the meaning and expression of others, and to compare their evaluation with the evaluation of others. Social workers know of some of the means to this end – different forms of consultation, groups and training – and have developed towards it a predictably ambivalent attitude. This ambivalence stems from the current incompleteness of these practices, for an emphasis upon the worker's self-awareness, though necessary, is insufficient, not only because 'the boundaries of self-knowledge have in the past been too narrowly drawn' (Timms and Timms, 1977), but also because the quality and use of the worker's awareness has been insufficiently evaluated.

One task in social work must be to widen the boundaries of personal awareness, an object in which the critical use of literature may perhaps play a part. But such use, it must be noted, will be a 'critical' use, and such use therefore suggests the demands which good practice places not only upon the worker but upon the worker's colleagues. It is at the root of good practice, critical practice, not only that the worker must 'analyse' but that he must 'compare', and this necessary comparison of literature serves as an example of the comparative procedure which must be the real basis of established competence in social work. Social workers must *know* of their ability to articulate and to evaluate meaning, and they can do so only by giving, receiving and comparing criticism with others. This need has specific institutional implications. It means that social workers must have easily available 'practice libraries', in writing and on tape, which will be the work examples for critical comparison. It means too that workers must, in detail, articulate and compare their critical approach to these examples and develop the procedures to do so. It means that social workers must prepare their own work examples, in writing, on tape and in simulation, and search out the detailed critical evaluation of their colleagues. It means that social workers must learn to offer constructive but precise evaluation of the work of others, and then compare their evaluations with the evaluations of others. It means too that these procedures, modelled by a published critical literature, confirmed by an explicit consultation with the client, must become the constant core procedures of professional development in social work, routinely and regularly undertaken through the worker's professional life. Such substantial, detailed appraisal of practice will be unfamiliar and taxing to the worker and will also make demands upon agency time and the structure of professional relationships, but these are necessary demands and must be included as conditions of the professional role. The procedures must be recognized by education and practice agencies as the only route in social work towards something 'which may provisionally be called truth'.

But no procedures, and no theory and no art, are at root enough really to sustain the worker. Good social workers offer trust and concern, and are moved by a loving rather than a material interest in their fellow man, and it is this deeply personal commitment which ultimately constitutes the reward as well as the demand of social work. Social workers know that intimate meaning and experience must be shared and confirmed to promote well-being, yet there seems at present to be within many agencies an ethos more of distrust than trust, more of reserve than compassion. This may be because the style of relationships within highly stratified organizations is genuinely inimical to the necessary trust and sharing which social work demands, or it may be because social workers have not been able to establish the necessary professional language, communication and culture. But social workers cannot long love without being loved, they cannot long recognize the experience of others while their own experience remains unrecognized. Good practice, critical practice, in social work makes stringent demands upon the person of the worker, but it also recognizes that workers must give to each other a respect and care no less than they would give their clients. Good practice, critical practice, requires this precise attention upon the person of the worker; it also offers the ways and means by which such attention can be given.

PART 3

Showing the Way: Evaluating Social Work Practice

10

On Proving the Pudding: Steps in Social Work Criticism

THE CHALLENGE FOR THE CRITIC

This is intended to be a practical book. Readers impatient with abstraction and with theory may have been discouraged by the preceding chapters, and there is certainly an evident irony in writing of the urgent need for the personal and the concrete in social work literature and then writing so much which is itself impersonal and abstract. But it seemed that that path was one which had to be followed if the legitimacy, the necessity, of the personal and the concrete was to be properly established. The task now is to give substance to the preceding discussion, and to locate it in the reality of social work. For the only utility of the argument lies in its relevance for practice.

This book has so far laboured to reach conclusions which have sometimes seemed very familiar. I state this without apology, for it has been a necessary exploration. The arguments have needed 'not introduction, but an adequate priority', and the presentation of those conclusions has been necessary to ensure that they may come to be given a proper emphasis. Foremost amongst those conclusions is the assertion that the practice of social work must be evaluated, that it must be subject to a description and analysis which can determine quality. The principal value of identifying social work as art is that good social work (and bad social work) can be made visible and distinct. Such a claim invites demonstration and it is the purpose of this final section to constitute the first steps in that demonstration. It is in approaching this task that I do feel something more like apology – or if not apology, at least a marked diffidence; it seems a much more daunting business than the establishment of the argument on which the task is based.

One strand in this diffidence is that the reader may see the demonstration as the 'proof of the pudding', as the only test of my argument's utility. But there is a still more personal concern. In the discussion of detailed examples of social work practice my own judgement, and thus my own person, must be itself much more open to scrutiny and assessment, for the only route to the description and the evaluation of social work lies in the declaration of imagination and personal response. So my diffidence demonstrates one of the difficulties and constraints in developing good and critical practice in social work: that the necessity for this implicit declaration of self demands that the worker and the critic be open to the consequent possibility of a personal challenge and rejection. I have at least the small consolation that in fact the exercise does not constitute the final proving of the pudding. It may be that I fail to show myself an able creator or critic and so that I cast doubt upon my likely competence as a social worker. This would be no small matter in itself, but it would not disprove the thesis about the general character of competence in social work. My argument could still be judged sound, but not my own ability to fulfil the conditions it imposes.

These disclaimers indicate a change of gear. The sections which follow point the way towards a creative and a critical literature in social work and seek to give briefly some preliminary idea of the way in which such a literature could be developed. They offer material which is very different in kind from the material in the first two parts of this book. Each section comprises an account of social work practice prepared by a worker, together with a critical discussion of the work in which I attempt to understand and to determine its quality. This procedure requires a much more active relationship with the reader as criticism requires not only analysis but comparison, and so my task becomes a more immediately discursive one: to clarify my own response so that (adapting Leavis's phrase) others can then interrogate their own experience to see if the essential order looks like that to them also. Such a process has obvious parallels with the reader's response to theoretical argument – the reader will reflect upon the extent of his own agreement – but it differs in two important ways. First, in criticism, critic and reader are both responding to a shared and very specific stimulus – they both read the same account. Secondly, the stimulus is one which necessarily demands of them the fullness of an aesthetic response, rather than one which is mainly intellectual. Effective criticism thus has the character of a much more personal encounter.

It is likely that the material which follows will seem to the reader more colloquial in style than the preceding sections, more ordinary and familiar. It should be closer to the stuff of daily practice. If it is, it then lies close to the kernel of this whole inquiry: it gives access to crucial questions about the essential character of social work practice and, more important still, to the possibility of identifying quality in practice. The material will also seem familiar because most social workers during their own student days (and these are student accounts) will have prepared and evaluated such detailed reports of practice; the manner of the material, to a point at least, is not new. But the procedures required by a critical practice, it has already been explained, *are* familiar ones and this familiarity includes the manner in which accounts of practice must be treated. The difficulty is that such procedures have no adequate hold in the general practice of social work. It is to the cost of social work that the creative and the critical experience required in such accounts is mainly confined to the professional foothills of the qualifying courses. There can be no hope of climbing to any greater sophistication in either descriptive or critical approaches to social work unless such treatments become the object of much wider professional debate and development.

The accounts of practice which follow describe apparently effective social work. They have been selected because each illustrates a markedly different approach to the problem of describing social work. It becomes clear that, in different ways, the first and second accounts actually preclude a real evaluation, while the approach used in the third makes possible a much more plausible access to the strengths and weaknesses of the practice it describes. The consideration of these accounts makes clear the emphasis which must necessarily be found at the centre of good practice, and of good descriptions of practice.

In the accounts, names and certain details have been obscured to ensure the anonymity of the people involved. Each account describes the work of a social worker in an area office of a local authority social services department.

SOCIAL WORK WITH A SINGLE PARENT FAMILY

THE ACCOUNT WRITTEN BY THE SOCIAL WORKER

Initial information and social work history

Ms Kennedy is a 22-year-old single parent with son Peter, aged 2. Ms Kennedy was originally referred to a hospital social work department three years ago when she was attending the antenatal clinic prior to Peter's birth. The presenting problems were then housing and financial difficulties, as Ms Kennedy had recently come north from a hostel for single pregnant girls in London. Prior to the pregnancy she had been living in London with Peter's father, a Nigerian, but she was rejected by him when he learned of the pregnancy. Ms Kennedy is Irish and in contact with her family of origin, but they are all living in Ireland.

Peter was born by Caesarian section. The birth was difficult and soon after birth Peter was diagnosed as having a heart condition. The baby was kept in special care for six weeks and this early separation of mother and child precipitated bonding problems which, after Ms Kennedy's hospital discharge, were soon noted by the health visitor. Social Services (from another borough) were involved in the first six months of Peter's life as the medical problems seemed to be accentuating the difficulties Ms Kennedy was experiencing in coping alone with a newborn child. During these six months, the baby was readmitted twice to hospital (with pneumonia and asthma) and Peter was twice received into voluntary care because Ms Kennedy was expressing an inability to care for him. Eighteen months ago Ms Kennedy moved to this part of the midlands. Since then, she has experienced numerous housing and financial problems, being evicted twice. Social Services became involved again nine months ago when Ms Kennedy was requesting a day nursery place for her child and help in paying massive electricity debts. When I assumed responsibility for this case, five months ago, in January, Ms Kennedy was facing another eviction, and Peter was awaiting a nursery place.

Financial situation

Ms Kennedy claims Supplementary Benefit and a Single Parent Child Benefit. Other than that she has no separate income nor savings.

Housing

At the time of case transfer Ms Kennedy was living in private rented accommodation alone with Peter. The flat was on the first floor and she was paying rent to the owner of the flat below, whom she believed to be the owner of the whole property.

Social network

Ms Kennedy has a boyfriend in the neighbouring borough but contact is irregular due both to distance and the fact of his working shifts. He seems to offer Ms Kennedy adequate support and relates well to Peter, but Ms Kennedy is reluctant to enter into a marriage although that is what he desires. Ms Kennedy's family are all in Ireland and maintain regular contact, although there was initial conflict surrounding Peter's illegitimacy (the family being RC). At the time of transfer, Ms Kennedy and Peter were in Ireland spending a week with the family. Other than her boyfriend, Ms Kennedy only has a few friends living locally and, overall, appears very vulnerable. According to previous social work assessments, she has been seen as particularly prone to depression and the anxieties of loneliness.

Initial analysis

At the transfer stage, the presenting problems seemed twofold. First, there were housing and financial difficulties surrounding an imminent eviction and secondly, there seemed more long-term anxieties surrounding Ms Kennedy's vulnerability and lack of confidence in coping alone with her 2-year-old son.

The housing crisis became the most immediate issue since at the transfer visit it transpired that on her return from Ireland Ms Kennedy was faced with an eviction order. As mentioned above, she had been paying rent to the owner of the flat below in good faith that he was the owner, whereas in fact Ms Kennedy was a sub-tenant as the whole property was owned by a third party. The third party had obtained a possession order and the eviction order was imminent. Thus at the transfer visit I was faced with a crisis and that afternoon accompanied Ms Kennedy to an emergency appointment with the Housing Department who were fortunately admitting their liability to house Ms Kennedy and Peter.

In relation to a more overall assessment of Ms Kennedy the most obvious danger in subsequent work seemed to be a possible over-dependence on social work help. In the past it seems likely that Peter's two fortnight breaks in voluntary care had undermined Ms Kennedy's confidence in her ability as mother. They were a sign that she had failed. At the transfer stage she certainly exhibited a low level of self-esteem and self-confidence and her emotional vulnerability seemed aggravated by a poor supportive social network. Yet coupled with this vulnerability appeared also an ability to manipulate professional workers into assuming responsibility for some of the housing and financial problems that she should have faced herself. A mixture of bad luck and poor management seemed to have been responsible for the two past evicitons and the constant changes of address have had an unsettling effect on both Ms Kennedy and Peter, acting against the establishment of a securing routine.

With reference specifically to Peter, he presents as an extremely active child (despite the medical history), but liable to temper tantrums which seem in part a product of sensed anxiety toward his mother's lack of confidence in coping with him. (Recent research on asthmatic attacks in children has pointed to the significance of mother–child bonding in stimulating such conditions.) Ms Kennedy's early separation from Peter does seem significant in understanding their current relationship as does also an appreciation of Ms Kennedy's attitude to her loss of independence and the subsequent restrictions of single parenting. Ms Kennedy's relationship with Peter appears ambivalent, as she both loves and resents the child. There is no contact at all with

Peter's father, but as the pregnancy was unplanned and initially unwanted some of the resentment, anger and unhappiness felt towards the boyfriend's rejection seems to have been projected on to the child. Peter's subsequent medical problems at birth caused an early separation of mother and son which hampered the development of a close, nurturing relationship. Ms Kennedy's accompanying guilt surrounding Peter's illegitimacy and her anxiety in accepting her child's medical condition seem also significant factors. In the current relationship, resentment still exists in the sense that Ms Kennedy would prefer to work and have more money for clothes and nights out than her Supplementary Benefit will permit. Yet in the face of this ambivalence Ms Kennedy does care deeply for her child and will panic easily if he is sick or she cannot control his tantrums. A possible difficulty is the fact that she possesses rather idealistic notions about parenting and indeed about life, and becomes upset and disillusioned when these fail to materialize, as for example with expectations of housing, financial allowance, availability of part-time work and regular baby sitters.

Intervention

Thus in relation to this initial assessment two areas of concern were noted. At the transfer visit Ms Kennedy was enthusiastic concerning my involvement but, as has also been noted, I was aware of her adopting a position of learned helplessness (see Seligman, 1975). The housing crisis necessitated immediate action and a task-centred approach seemed the most appropriate, but for the more long-term work of support and guidance with the mother-child relationship this would require the more gradual development of a trusting relationship. Liaison with external agencies such as the day nursery would also be envisaged for the parenting and support work. The day nursery seemed particularly appropriate since Peter's speech was underdeveloped for his age (according to the Stycar developmental sequence; Sheridan, 1975). In response to this, the nursery would offer both the stimulation and socialization that Ms Kennedy would find it difficult to offer Peter on her own. As a result of a new initiative from the nursery towards increasing the involvement of parents in nursery care, Peter's attendance would help rather than hinder the parental relationship, although also offering Ms Kennedy a break.

At the beginning of intervention my plan and objectives were therefore as follows:

(1) To develop a trusting relationship with Ms Kennedy and Peter without creating an unwanted and unhelpful dependency. In particular I was aware of the possibility of manipulation and did not want to allow Ms Kennedy to assume a position of learned helplessness.

(2) To offer advice and support to Ms Kennedy and Peter in relation to welfare benefits and their housing and financial situation. In this I was also anticipating an advocacy role in negotiating with both the DHSS and Housing Department.

(3) Within the trusting relationship (1 above) to offer regular support to Ms Kennedy and more specifically to explore both her feelings and responses to single parenting.

(4) To encourage Ms Kennedy to develop a more supportive social network by offering contacts with local single parent organizations.

(5) To establish good liaison with the day nursery and Ms Kennedy's health visitor.

The work with Ms Kennedy on her relationship with Peter and the work building up Ms Kennedy's confidence and competence in coping alone would obviously involve long-term supportive contact. However, in relation to the more immediate housing and financial crises short-term targets were anticipated to relieve immediate pressure. Our meetings began weekly, but towards the end of the time the visits became less frequent. As my work was for a defined period of time it was important to clarify this at the beginning of the contract so that feelings of loss could be anticipated and the question of a suitable replacement worker also considered.

In retrospect, five distinctive stages may be identified in my intervention. These stages developed in response to five clearly defined crises which arose in the life of Ms Kennedy. In dealing with them the long-term objectives outlined above were not jettisoned, but rather seen as relevant goals to help overcome the more immediate problem. Dealing with a succession of crises in fact accelerated the establishment of a functional trust relationship between myself and Ms Kennedy and also provided a focus for exploration of Ms Kennedy's feelings and responses towards single parenting. The five stages of intervention will be summarized in their chronological order.

Housing – January: initial six weeks

As outlined above, at my transfer visit with Ms Kennedy's former social worker we were faced with an imminent eviction and I accompanied her to the Housing Department. As a result of this visit Ms Kennedy and Peter were promised temporary bed and breakfast accommodation from the following Monday. Transport and furniture storage were arranged, and the following week they moved into a single DHSS bedsit.

Specific action   During these six weeks my role was both that of advocate and supportive social worker. I negotiated with the DHSS, a local voluntary housing organization and the Housing Department to check the legal situation on eviction and also to request help with Ms Kennedy's removal expenses and the court costs incurred in losing the possession order. The legal situation was more complex since Ms Kennedy was actually a sub-tenant. No financial assistance was available from the DHSS. Consequently, I contacted three independent local charities for help and as a result the court debt was cleared out of court. During this period Peter started nursery two days per week.

Analysis   During this period my input was intense in response particularly to the housing crisis and Ms Kennedy's subsequent depression. The move to a small and sparsely furnished room with a highly active child resulted in Ms Kennedy feeling increasingly stressed, anxious and vulnerable. The lack of space was causing her to feel near to the limits of coping with Peter. The resultant stress was picked up by the toddler who responded with tantrums. Ms Kennedy visited her GP who prescribed librium, but my emphasis was upon building up a more supportive network. Ms Kennedy's boyfriend was helpful and Ms Kennedy could spend weekends there, but mid-week the pressure became more acute. In liaison with the health visitor we negotiated a joint programme of visiting and I suggested a mother and toddler group. Work by the health visitor and myself was consistent with my long-term goals and was more specifically concerned with helping Ms Kennedy both understand and handle her child's tantrums. The day nursery offered an important break for Ms Kennedy two days per week. In relation to the long-term housing problem, supportive letters were written on Ms Kennedy's behalf to the Housing Department from the relevant GP, health visitor and myself. At the end of this period, Ms Kennedy remained in temporary accommodation, but her life was structured more to cope with the additional stress.

Fuel Debts; end February

At this stage I was visiting weekly and Ms Kennedy was seeming less depressed, although still obviously apprehensive about the time lapse before she would be rehoused. However, at one visit in this period she informed me that she had received a large bill from the electricity board for past fuel debts. The debt was incurred at a former address when Ms Kennedy lived in a shared house and had inadvertently assumed responsibility to pay the fuel bills. The others in the house had left without addresses and Ms Kennedy was left responsible for the whole amount.

Specific action   In responding to such debts it was important for Ms Kennedy not to offload responsibility, so the problem was tackled by simple task setting. She agreed to contact the electricity board about instalment payment and also to attempt to contact the former occupants of the shared house. I also verified the legal situation. The current situation, however, remains that the debts are unpaid because the electricity board are still investigating.

Analysis   During this stage Ms Kennedy seemed to be coping better with a confined space and also feeling happier controlling Peter. The revelation of the fuel debt was a disappointment, but it also emphasized Ms Kennedy's vulnerability and naivety. At this stage the visits were continuing weekly.

Health problems – mid-March

At a visit in mid-March I found Ms Kennedy frantic about her own state of health. She had been menstruating continuously for the previous three weeks and was naturally feeling extremely tired and worried by hair falling out and weight loss. She was naturally anxious about the possibility of cancer. In response to this, I urged the importance of seeing her GP although she was reluctant to do so. However, before she saw the GP, Peter was admitted to hospital following an asthmatic attack. He was kept in hospital for ten days. During this week Ms Kennedy visited the hospital daily, but also saw her own GP. The tablets he prescribed, however, were not dispensed since the chemist refused to do so on the basis that they had been banned some years previously.

Specific action I felt appalled at the standard of health treatment from Ms Kennedy's GP, and went with her to the GP to ask for a hospital gynaecological appointment in view of his obsolete prescription. This was readily obtained. I also contacted the hospital for reports on Peter and the health visitor for reassurance concerning Ms Kennedy's own state of health.

Analysis Although an extremely anxious period for Ms Kennedy and Peter, this time was particularly valuable for looking more closely at the parent–child relationship. In Peter's absence, Ms Kennedy was wanting to talk about their early bonding difficulties. The recent period of hospitalization had crystallized her feelings toward Peter and she was wanting to explore them. This led into a discussion about her ex-boyfriend and her feelings toward him. She has decided definitely against marriage to her current boyfriend but instead wanted to consider extending her social network. Hence she made contact with the local organization for single parents. At the end of this period Ms Kennedy's parents and sister visited from Ireland, which increased her morale enormously.

Peter's reception into care; end April
Peter was received into care (1980 Child Care Act, Section 2) on a day when I was away from the office, after Ms Kennedy had abandoned him at the Housing Department following an argument over the question of rehousing. The Housing Department had called Social Services, but Ms Kennedy was not contactable. Peter was placed with short-term foster parents. Ms Kennedy was seen the following day by the duty social worker.

Specific action I contacted Ms Kennedy on my return and thought her to be depressed, but also confronted her with using Peter as a pawn to quicker rehousing. The interview was extremely long and intense, with Ms Kennedy saying she needed to see a psychiatrist. What had provoked her to abandon Peter was that she had seen a number of beetles in her room, panicked and went to the Housing Department. Abandoning him had been pre-meditated, but she had apparently received psychiatric help in the past for a spider phobia. Although very conscious of the dangers of drift in child care we agreed that Peter should stay with foster parents for a week and in return Ms Kennedy agreed to visit him. This was initially difficult because of the mother's shame, anxiety and confusion about what would be best for her child. Meanwhile, my work was extended to supervising Peter's foster parents who were very accepting and non-judgemental concerning contact from Peter's mother. Peter returned home a week later as I had negotiated two important changes to reduce Ms Kennedy's anxiety level:

(1) First, I made a referral (with Ms Kennedy's approval) to a local centre for the mentally ill for a supportive mental health programme.
(2) Secondly, I negotiated with the nursery for Peter to attend full-time and for Ms Kennedy also to become more involved in shared care at the nursery.

Analysis Peter's reception into care was unfortunate both in itself and in the fact that I was away from the agency. Ms Kennedy had been untraceable immediately after abandoning Peter because she had gone to her GP. However, the whole event illustrated both Ms Kennedy's fragile mental health and her ability to manipulate others. My predicament as worker was that I sympathized with her anger towards Housing yet could not condone her desperate action. In responding to her emotional state I was aware that more support and psychiatric help were required, yet also confident that I had to be honest about the possible consequences of such an action (formal care proceedings). It was fortunate that Ms Kennedy's sister was staying with her during the crisis. After Peter's return home, Ms Kennedy seemed calmer and relieved about the extra days at the nursery and the referral to the centre for herself.

Suspected non-accidental injury

This does not really comprise a separate issue, but it suggests the importance of specialist knowledge relating to multi-racial health problems. Whilst Peter was with foster parents they noticed an area of old small bruises on the base of the spine. They immediately notified the duty social services team and the child was examined by a GP who identified extensive bruising. This occurred while I was away and upon my return I was consequently greeted with a panic about possible child abuse. However, known to me in the case notes was reference to a skin pigmentation condition prevalent in mixed race babies. The note was consistent with the location of the 'bruising' on Peter's back. Therefore I rang the GP who had raised the alarm. He was very sceptical, having not heard of the condition. Thus I had to contact a consultant and the Social Services Department from Ms Kennedy's former local authority. Eventually, the GP accepted the diagnosis and I was satisfied on seeing the child. However, the whole alarm could have been spared if the condition had been recorded on the child's medical record.

The current position is that Ms Kennedy and Peter are still in temporary accommodation, but are supposedly at the top of the housing list. Peter is attending nursery daily and Ms Kennedy becoming more involved. This is having a definite effect on his speech development. Ms Kennedy is feeling calmer and less prone to depression, feeling her support structure to be improved and that she is less restricted with a daily break from Peter and the single room. Mother and child seem to be relating better and there have been no further asthmatic attacks. Ms Kennedy is awaiting an appointment with the mental health centre.

Evaluation of intervention

This case has incorporated numerous diverse components. Yet although from my summary it may appear that work has simply gone from crisis to crisis, in so doing long-term work has been performed and progress achieved towards my initial long-term goals.

In relation to my first objective a trusting relationship may be seen to have developed between Ms Kennedy and myself. This has facilitated the honest exploration of feelings and responses and also permitted me to confront Ms Kennedy's attempts at manipulation on a number of occasions.

Secondly, in relation to housing and financial advice, contact was frequently made with both DHSS and Housing and legal advice obtained as required. In this my role was very much that of advocate.

Thirdly, in relation to work on parenting, liaison with Ms Kennedy's health visitor and the nursery enabled me to tackle the various problems of child handling and confidence with the support of the other two agencies. One of my chief obstacles in this work was Ms Kennedy's idealism and initial naivety about parenting. Rather unreal expectations about a luxurious house, garden, job and lifestyle at first impeded progress because it placed all the responsibility for Ms Kennedy's unhappiness on the housing situation. While this was indeed the most oppressing factor Ms Kennedy's recurring resentment towards Peter is also the consequence of unresolved feelings toward his father and poor provision for single parents. The current relationship between Ms Kennedy and Peter seems identifiably much closer than at first and this seems in part a product of the crises they have endured together. Ms Kennedy has now begun to think more positively towards the future.

Fourthly, in relation to improving Ms Kennedy's social network she has established links with two single parent organizations and the nursery. Attendance at the mental health centre remains in the pipeline.

Fifthly and finally, liaison with the nursery and the health visitor was throughout viewed as important, facilitating an information exchange between the three parties.

My work with this family has followed a definite sequence of crisis and calm. Yet in the last visits a more intensive supportive structure has been incorporated into Ms Kennedy's lifestyle which has been experienced by her as valuable. At my most recent visit my leaving was discussed. It was felt to be significant that Ms Kennedy was looking towards the future in new accommodation and also envisaging the eventual redundancy of social work input.

End of the account written by the social worker. (The references cited in the account are included in the general list of references at the end of the book.)

DISCUSSION

One simple virtue of this account, in this context, is its length. The worker has written more fully than most social workers would have time or appropriate opportunity to match. Social work needs some accounts which are bigger than present conventions allow. Routine records and reports rightly require brevity, but there must exist in social work accounts which offer greater detail and variety; indeed, there will be a place for the book which is entirely a narrative of social work practice. It is a merit of this account that it has the substance to give scope for comment and comparison.

But social work will be measured not by its quantity but by its quality. This account is distinct because of its character. It is distinct particularly in its diversity, in its report of the complexity of influences, problems and perceptions to which the worker must give recognition. It is a diversity which will be readily familiar to most social workers, who deal routinely with, for example, the simultaneous pressures of poverty, homelessness, depression, isolation, race and immaturity, all of which are relevant in this situation. Published accounts of social work often fail to reflect this diversity. They are frequently chosen to illustrate one selected theme, not to show the complexity which must universally characterize experience. So it is a major merit of this account that it gives some clue to that complexity.

The account has other merits. It shows, for example, something of the way in which the worker's analysis attempts to give shape to her information about her client, it points to her tentative exploration of some sources of her learning, and it describes the principal procedural steps which she has taken. These unfortunately are not reliably routine features of reports of social work. The account also gives some indication of changes that occur in the client's circumstances. Social work is primarily a problem-solving process and it is a requirement of an account of practice that change, or its absence, be identified. Even good social work may not be able to achieve change, but a good account must always permit evaluation of the extent to which it is achieved.

It is, however, in this need to evaluate that it is first possible to see the ways in which this account is incomplete or misconceived. The task is to evaluate social work practice, and so, in this instance, to determine whether the worker plausibly and adequately helped this family. We know something of the worker's understanding of the steps she took to help and a little to suggest the clients' improved well-being. Do we then know enough properly to evaluate the work? The answer, I suggest, is that we do not. We can, as will be seen later, *infer* something of the likely good quality of this work, but the account – and probably the work itself – fails at root to offer an adequately integrated description of the situation. It does not make clear the links between understanding, action and effect; the clients' improved well-being is not ultimately shown to be rooted in the worker's practice.

This may seem a hard judgement. The worker is clearly energetic on her clients' behalf, and her efforts are plausibly varied and imaginative – for example, she arranges accommodation, visits the doctor, constructively challenges Ms Kennedy about her behaviour towards Peter (and therefore fosters the trust which permits this), supervises foster parents, and keeps a watchful eye on Peter's developmental progress. There is clearly no lack of activity. She also reports on beneficial change: that Peter's speech and health have improved, that Ms Kennedy is calmer, less prone to feelings of depression and restriction, that mother and child relate better to each other, that the family is ('supposedly' – a rather sinister qualification) at the top of the housing list. Ms Kennedy herself experiences the changes as valuable. It all seems an impressive catalogue.

But it is clear that the worker herself has misgivings about her account of her work. The report of action taken – some half of the text – does not just take account of the crises which occurred, but is organized around them. The worker is uneasy about this. She adopts a rather apologetic tone as she introduces the 'Intervention' section: that 'In dealing with [the crises] the long-term objectives ... were not jettisoned'; she knows that in structuring the account around hurdles negotiated it becomes an inadequate representation of what actually happened. She notes after the narrative is concluded that 'from my summary it may appear that the work has simply gone from crisis to crisis', by implication stating that the work has not 'simply' followed such a course. She tries to retrieve this situation by referring to her original goals and noting the relevant changes that have occurred. This is inevitably an unsatisfactory procedure. It identifies objectives and outcomes, but offers no scope for linking the two; the manner in which change is achieved is not discussed. It is almost (but not quite) as if, as so often in social work, things somehow just happen.

The account illustrates the difficulty which social workers have even in describing practice, and without adequate description there can be no possibility of evaluation. The worker believes that relevant and effective work has been done but she fails to substantiate the relevance of that work. There is evidence of change, and there are, as will be seen, suggestions of apparently appropriate sensitivity and purpose, but the link between the two is only an implied link. The account has complexity but it lacks an adequate coherence, or a properly established focus. It is this failing which obscures the determination of any plausible connection between the worker's efforts and the outcome of her work. It is the character of this omission which has to be explored to understand why this work cannot be the subject of any real evaluation.

This account fails because it leaves out of account an adequate picture of coping, meaning and understanding. The worker's 'analysis' falls far short of making clear the character of this particular situation, which could only be realized by the inclusion of information about Ms Kennedy's capacity to cope and, in turn, about the meaning Ms Kennedy herself gives to her situation. In other words, the worker gives very little idea of what Ms Kennedy is like as a person. The information which is given is relevant and intelligible, but it is insufficient; the worker's understanding is almost certainly (because of her apparent effect) informed by a much more intimate and individualized sense of Ms Kennedy's experience, but this sense is not reported. Yet it is only this information which will define the real character of the problem. The account fails because it does not include pictures of how Ms

Kennedy preceives and explains her problems, of how she copes, or of the ways in which Ms Kennedy feels that her problems might be solved.

Coping and meaning are accessible only through a process of understanding, of 'sympathetic insight into the mental life of other people', and this demands the imaginative engagement of the worker. The account therefore fails because it does not make clear the character of the worker's own experience in this situation; she leaves out not only the client but herself. It may be possible to infer the vitality and imagination of the worker's engagement, because of the apparent achievement of trust and change, but this engagement is barely reported. The account is thus rendered two dimensional, it fails to reflect the human nature of a human encounter. In short, it lacks an account of intuition and the worker's use of self.

It is this omission – of the worker herself – which is the missing centre of the report. Social work is a problem-solving process which requires that the worker state clearly the nature of the problem she perceives and the goal of her professional effort. The worker's failure to give, literally, a proper account of herself means that she omits not only to describe her initial understanding of her client, but also to make properly clear the various stages of her subsequent understanding and action. It means that her analysis is not open to any confirmation, that her definition of the problem is unclear and that, in consequence, the account of her objectives and her intervention are seriously weakened. The ommission can be shown to pervade the whole sequence of the report.

The worker's failure to represent her experience in understanding accounts for her difficulty in giving coherence to the complexity of her material. The worker makes a selection from a potentially limitless range of information about her client. She may know in advance that a certain area of information (for example, 'guilt surrounding . . . illegitimacy') may be relevant, but she can give it weight only if it proves in fact to be an issue for this client. The priority, as always, can only be the relative significance of events in the world of this particular family. The worker considers a range of diverse issues – for example, wealth, culture, biography, personality – but they are useful only in the particular way they inform her understanding of this client's experience and this client's capacity to cope. But the worker gives little indication of how she selects and shapes this material. It appears somehow as a given quantity, even though it can only be an expression of the worker's intuitive knowledge and can be evaluated only if she describes the manner of its achievement.

This weakness in the 'analysis' makes for predictable difficulty in clearly identifying the problems which the worker must seek to resolve. The worker explains too little of her own concerns and priorities. Her role as a social services worker requires her to give first place to Peter's welfare and it is evidently her assessment that his welfare will be best served by continuing but improved care from his mother. It is perhaps not surprising that this assessment is left implicit. But it is a major omission that the worker does not make explicit that it is a problem of inadequate parental coping which she comes to define as her *principal* concern. It is clear in the 'Initial analysis' and the first paragraph of the 'Intervention' sections that the worker is focusing primarily upon Ms Kennedy's capacity to cope adequately as a parent. Yet the problem is sometimes discussed as if it had equal emphasis with another problem, housing. These are in fact problems of a different order and it follows from the agency's role that housing, although clearly a crucial matter, is relevant for this worker because of its importance for Peter's welfare. Coping is really the worker's priority for, on those occasions when she does assert a dual focus on housing and parenting, the discussion about parenting is always given a greater length and emphasis. It therefore seems possible to conclude that the worker does intend to focus her effort upon coping, upon Ms Kennedy's capacity to cope with her responsibilities as Peter's mother. But she does not state this focus with the necessary unambiguous clarity.

The uncertainty about coping as the focal problem reflects the general difficulty found in social work of making use of coping as a central organizing concept. It has become clear that coping is an elusive and an imprecise concept which offers nothing of the satisfying objective certainty which social work may seek. In consequence, social workers themselves often seem to find it difficult to grasp or articulate their real purpose. To understand and to influence coping is a process which demands of the worker that purposeful use of self which has been seen to arouse such ambivalence in social work. In this account the ambiguity is such that the worker fails almost entirely to make explicit the central problem – Ms Kennedy's capacity to cope as a parent – in her list of objectives, which (accepting the worker's assumption that Ms Kennedy *can* be helped to cope better as Peter's parent) should be dominated by a primary objective of 'improved parental coping'.

This omission is almost certainly responsible for the implausibility of the 'plan and objectives' outlined early in the 'Intervention' section. The worker identifies her goals as the establishment of a trusting relationship, the offering of benefits advice, the exploration of the client's role as parent, the development of social support, and maintaining inter-agency liaison. This is not a helpful list. It fails not because its contents are irrelevant but because of confusion. The confusion lies in the failure to differentiate 'ultimate' objectives – exploring 'feelings and responses to ... parenting' (which presumably stands for the worker's implicit goal of improved parental coping) and, in the worker's view, housing – from 'instrumental' objectives – making the relationship, increasing social support, inter-agency liaison (and, in my view, housing), which are the means by which the ultimate objectives will be realized. The confusion stems from the failure to recognize the priority of coping and thus from the worker's reluctance to give proper emphasis to intuition and to the use of self. It is this confusion, this lack of coherence, which obscures the clarity of the remainder of the account.

The worker's failure to incorporate an account of intuition means that she does not, and perhaps cannot, make her work adequately specific and detailed. To be of most practical use her objectives must become much more behaviourally and temporally exact. In 'task-centred' terms (Reid and Epstein, 1972) the worker must have some means of knowing precisely what it is that she and the client are going to try to do, and when they are going to try to do it. The given list of objectives does not lend itself to such specificity; it can hardly do so if the worker's earlier analysis has failed to define the problem properly. The impossibility of this specific material precludes the possibility of specific evaluation. The worker claims that her intervention is effective, but she cannot possibly show the extent of this effect or explain its realization.

It is a consequence of this lack of specific focus that the remainder of the account lacks an appropriate structure. It is because of the apparent vacuum in the worker's thinking that she builds her account of her intervention around the five crises. It is no surprise that these crises dominate the experience of the work, and constitute its temporal stages, but they are presented as if they were the organizing features of the work itself. The rather rueful tone, noted previously, which the worker adopts at the end of her account points to her own misgivings about this emphasis in her description. It occurs because of the confusion in her objectives; they can offer no appropriate structure around which to organize the work, and in the consequent uncertainty the worker and the client are dominated by events. This seems to be the familiar experience of social work, the routine lament that social work is 'crisis oriented'. This is not crisis in the constructive sense of Parad's (1965) 'crisis intervention'. 'Crisis intervention' theory in fact lends itself very well to an emphasis upon the concepts of meaning and coping, pointing to the way in which people subjected to the disequilibrium of loss and change make urgent attempts to create a new and stable understanding of the world. This is crisis in the sense of always chasing patchily from one crisis to another, offering only a breathless and minimal first-aid. This crisis orientation means a failure to establish a proper understanding and purpose, rooted in intuition, which in turn means that the structure of the work becomes haphazard, a matter (apparently) only of crisis and reaction to crisis. This account can therefore be seen to illustrate a familiar problem. It fails to give proper place to intuition, and in consequence it fails to achieve coherence in its account of purpose and practice.

This particular account has another value, however, because it also hints at the worker's *real* agenda, and so offers clues to the reason for her likely effect and the real character of her practice. The value of this account lies primarily in its demonstration of the elusiveness of intuition; it is not in fact an account of bad social work but an account which fails adequately to describe social work. It is a confusing account, suggesting substance and achievement, and yet on examination offering no real clarity about either. The worker seems to be effective and articulate, but her account fails to show the essence of her practice. Small wonder then that less able workers find themselves groping and confused, unable to locate the measures which will give them proper clarity and purpose.

I noted earlier that my comments may seem a hard judgement on this work. I think they have been too total a judgement. A reading of this account confuses because it gives clues about the likely competence and real focus of the worker's practice, but this competence and coherence are not properly anchored and explained. The account itself is not coherent, but the worker includes throughout her 'Intervention' sequence material which indicates the likely greater coherence of her practice. The apologetic tone of her conclusion – 'from my summary it may appear' – reflects not an afterthought, but a sense that the content of the account has not matched the structure of her practice. The account confuses because it offers glimpses of an entirely appropriate emphasis but then does not take proper responsibility for that emphasis. Indeed, the judgement may seem hard because this implicit emphasis is so appropriate that it is deceptively easy on preliminary reading to assume that it is in fact the explicit content.

The implicit emphasis permeates the sequence on the worker's activity and consistently confirms that her real objective is to improve Ms Kennedy's capacity to cope as Peter's mother. The worker states that the crises 'in fact accelerated the establishment of a functional trust relationship' between herself and Ms Kennedy and 'provided a focus for exploration of Ms Kennedy's feelings and responses towards single parenting'. This leaves no room for doubt about the real priority. But 'in fact' is a necessary justification, because the worker knows that the account's organization around the crises tends to obscure the priority of this focus. Her dependence upon the crises masks her real emphasis. Yet it can be seen that her real attention is upon issues of coping, meaning, and experience. The noted effect of 'housing' is that Ms Kennedy is 'stressed, anxious and vulnerable ... near to the limits of coping', the stress is 'picked up by the toddler', and attention is focused upon helping Ms Kennedy 'understand and handle her child's tantrums'. Discussion about 'fuel debts' in fact emphasizes that the worker's concern is not to assume the responsibility for coping, that the client feels better about her control of her son, and that the debts are an indication of

'vulnerability and naivety'. The period marked by 'health problems' is a time to talk about the experience of relationships with
child and adults.

Social work is often a matter of the commonplace and common
sense. The crises, major crises, that beset this client clearly
demand a practical and an immediate response. But the crises
alone are not, or should not be, the dominant determining
influence upon the worker's response. Without some broader
sense of priority, crisis-oriented social work must necessarily be
haphazard, and a haphazard response, by definition, cannot be
justified as serving the best interests of the client. Yet in this
account it is as if the context of each crisis is always obscured; the
crisis is in fact handled to ensure that a wider objective is realized,
but the presentation emphasizes primarily the crisis itself. Which
way then do we look – at the organization of the account, which
draws attention to one focus, or to the implied content, which
seems also to describe an unacknowledged other? This is the real
confusion.

This account obscures intuition, but it does not make it
invisible. There is an implied emphasis upon the personal significance and meaning of events to client and worker, which points
to the importance of intuitive knowledge and intuitive behaviour.
It thus suggests the likely priority of the worker's actual practice.
Detailed goals and efforts can only be effective in an exact and an
imaginative knowledge of the client which demands a genuinely
personal engagement. The worker gives clues about this intuitive
involvement, but she gives only clues. It is not the centre piece of
her presentation. She therefore makes it possible to guess at the
reasons for her apparent good effect, but only to guess. So the
account fails – albeit only just – to offer scope for real understanding and real evaluation.

The worker seems to strive, with misgivings, after an impersonality which she feels is somehow demanded but which does not in
fact fit her task. Consider the words of her conclusions: 'It was
felt to be significant that Ms Kennedy was looking towards the
future in new accommodation and also envisaging the eventual
redundancy of social work input.' This is hardly the language of
that imaginative vitality which will have given her personal and
effective rapport with her client. It points to the broader need:
accounts of social work, if they are to take us nearer to the

practice and thinking of the worker, will have to have a rather different focus and style.

SOCIAL WORK WITH A MOTHER AND HER CHILD

THE ACCOUNT WRITTEN BY THE SOCIAL WORKER

An interview at home

This case concerns a 36-year-old single woman, Mrs Ellis, and her 7-year-old son, Kevin. Her son has been picked up by the police on two occasions, wandering about in the early evening. On one occasion he was near home but upset, and on the other he was over a mile from home. The police are concerned about him and feel that Mrs Ellis is neglectful; they referred the case to this London Borough Social Services Department.

I have visited on several occasions and tried to set up activities for Kevin after school to give Mrs Ellis some support. She had recently broken two appointments with me and claimed that she had to go out. On my last visit I had arranged to take Kevin to a children's club to see if he liked it, but when I got there, they were both out. I felt that there was no point in continuing to work with them under these conditions and went to see her for a view to sorting it out or terminating the contact.

When I knocked on the door, Mrs Ellis shouted from inside 'Who is it?' very loudly and aggressively. I had to shout back my name. She came to the door and said 'Oh, it's you – come in.' I went in and sat down. Kevin was pumping up the wheel of a bicycle and the TV was on with the volume very loud.

Social Worker	'I called last Thursday to take Kevin to the children's club.'	
Mrs Ellis	'Yes – you left your gloves last time you came' (fumbling around for them and giving them to me).	She was avoiding my eyes and trying to change the subject.

SW   'Thank you. As I said I
            called last Thursday but you
            weren't here.'

Mrs E.   'I know – he went and   This was offhand and
            played football and I went   defiant.
            out with my friend.'

SW   'You made an arrangement
            to see me.'

Mrs E.   'I told you not to go out – I   I felt angry that she was
to Kevin   told you to wait for the   prepared to blame K.
            lady.'

Mrs E   'I can't help it if he wants to   He may have wanted to
to SW   play football – I can't keep   go out but she could have
            him in if he wants to go out.'   said no, and it doesn't
                                             account for the other two
                                             times.

SW   'There are several things
            you could have done. You
            could have told him to stay
            in.'

Mrs E.   'I told you to wait for the
            lady, you little bleeder.'

SW   'You could have waited for   I continued as though she
            me yourself or you could   hadn't interrupted.
            have left me a note.'

Mrs E.   'It's not my bloody fault he   She was still trying to
            goes off. I can't make him go   shift the responsibility to
            with you if he wants to play   K.
            football.'

SW	'I didn't make the arrangements with Kevin, I made it with you. It's the third time I've made an appointment with you and you haven't kept it. I had to make arrangements to have my own child looked after so that I could take Kevin to the club and you don't even bother to make sure he's here.'	I was trying to make the point that it was her responsibility and I was angry.
Mrs E.	'I suppose it was a bit selfish but he said he wanted to go out and my friend came and took me out.' To K.: 'I told you.'	She was softening a bit at this point but still making a last stab at blaming K.
SW to K.	'Do you want to go to the club?'	I wanted to clarify things with him.
K.	Playing with the bike and mumbling.	
SW	'I can't understand you, could you turn around, so that I can talk to you? I'll turn the TV down so that I can hear you.'	I got up and turned the TV down.
K.	Turned around but continued to pump the wheel.	He was seeing what he could get away with.
SW	'Will you put the pump down and talk to me, please?'	
K.	Put down the pump and looked at me.	
SW	'Is football every Thursday night?'	I spoke with him gently.

K.   'No, only sometimes, it's on   This was animated and
       Sundays as well, I can go on   friendly.
       Sundays.'

SW   'Do you want to go to the
       club?'

K.   'I want to see what it's like.'

SW   'Are you prepared to miss
       football on Thursday night
       to find out?'

K.   'I'll see.'   This remark reminded
                                       me of Mrs E.; also she
                                       hadn't given permission
                                       for a change of attitude.

SW   'I'm afraid that's not good
       enough. You have to decide
       now because I'm not pre-
       pared to come here if you're
       not going to be at home.
       You have to decide now if
       you want to try it and if you
       make an arrangement with
       me you have to keep it. If
       you would rather go to foot-
       ball, that's fine.'

K.   'I want to go.'

SW   'Where?'   I wasn't sure if he meant
                                       football.

K.   'To the club.'

SW   'OK. Now what about this
       lady who was going to meet
       you and possibly do some-
       thing with you once a week
       – do you want to meet her?'

K.   'What's she like?'

SW   'She's between 20 and 25
          and she has fair hair and I
          think she's nice. She has said
          that she would take you
          swimming once a week or
          do something else.'

K.   'OK.'

SW   'Does that mean you would
          like to meet her and see how
          you get on?'

K.   'Yes.'   This felt good, that K.
                                              was not just responding
                                              to pressure from me.

SW   'If I make another arrange-
          ment to take you and K. to
          the club, will you keep it?'

Mrs E.   'If he wants to go he can, but   I think she was threat-
          I can't keep him in if he   ened by K's capitulation.
          doesn't want to.'.

SW   'I'm not prepared to make
          another arrangement under
          those conditions, either you
          make a commitment to be
          here or I'm not coming
          again.'

Mrs E.   'Suit your bloody self then,   She sounded angry but
          don't come if you don't   didn't look it and I felt
          want to.'   she   was   bluffing.
                                            However, I thought she
                                            might get herself in a
                                            position she couldn't get
                                            out of.

SW	'Well, that's what I came here to talk about. You've broken three appointments and that says something about the way you feel about me. I feel very angry about the last time – I don't even work on Thursdays and I'm not prepared to give up any more of my time coming here when you're not in. If you don't want me to come any more we can decide that now.'	The loophole – I hoped.
Mrs E.	'I'm sure you see other people on Thursdays, not only me.'	This felt defensive but also wanting to know if I had put myself out for her.
SW	'No – I don't work on Thursdays.'	
Mrs E.	'It was selfish – I didn't think of leaving a note.'	I knew I got through to her.
SW	'Did you forget I was coming?'	More gently.
Mrs E.	'No, but it never crossed my mind to leave a note. You can't, here, anyway, someone might break in.'	This sounded genuine and clear.
SW	'All right – do you want Kevin to go to the club and go out with the volunteer?'	I was saying that I had stopped fighting with her.
Mrs E.	'Yes, I'll come up with you.'	She agreed to stop.
SW	'Well, I'm going to be away next week so it will have to be the week after that.'	This was a bit punitive, but also true.

Mrs E.   'That's fine by me.'

SW   'And you'll definitely be
          here?'

Mrs E.   Smiling. 'Yes, I promise.'

SW   'What about Kevin, do you
          want to go to the club the
          week after next?'

K.   'Yes.'
          I made the arrangements
          and talked to her about her
          gas bill which was unpaid.
          At the door I said (smiling),

SW   'I'll see you the week after   A joke to check out if she
          next and you'd better be   felt OK about the row.
          here.'

Mrs E.   Smiling. 'I will, I promise.' She did feel OK.

Analysis

I learned quite a lot about Mrs E. from this interview. First, she
does want some support as that was all she had to lose and that's
why she backed down. I was prepared to pull out and she knew it.
By the time I left I felt much more warmth coming from her. We
had cleared the air and set some boundaries in our relationship
that we could both be comfortable with. I was aware that
boundary setting was an important issue between us and that she
is unable to do it with me or K. I didn't like what she did with K.
and felt that it was indicative of a lack of respect for him. She
won't get him to be more responsible unless she learns to respect
him.

As far as K. is concerned I felt sure at the time that she was
blaming him for her own lack of consideration. As I was writing
this up, however, I felt some doubts about how he may be feeling.
He may just be keeping the peace by agreeing to go to the club and I
will be aware of this when I take him. On the other hand, I felt in
this interview, as I felt in the previous interview, that if you talk to
him calmly and listen to him he will readily tell you what he wants.

The visit to the club

When I arrived Mrs Ellis was waiting with her coat on and seemed pleased to see me. I drove them to the local community centre and introduced them to the person in charge of the children's club. Kevin joined in without difficulty and began to play games with the other children. Mrs Ellis and I sat on the sidelines to wait until Kevin had settled down and was confident enough to be left. I had arranged for Kevin to be taken home after the session. Mrs Ellis noticed a sheet pinned to the wall advertising a camping weekend for the children.

Mrs E. 'That's good, isn't it, they take them away camping. Kevin would love that.'

She seemed to be very impressed with the place and had said that she had never realized that a community centre existed.

SW 'We can find out if he can go.'

Mrs E. 'He'd like to go but what would I do?'

This felt as though they were both children and K. was going to get something that she wasn't.

SW 'You could have a weekend to yourself.'

I know that she enjoys socializing and thought it would give her a break.

Mrs E. 'I don't want that, I've never been parted from Kevin. I'd be frightened on my own. In those flats all sorts of things happen. I had a dosser sleeping on my roof last year. Then he got into my outhouse. I didn't even know he was there – Kevin found him. You can't trust anyone around the flats. I could be murdered in my bed. Sometimes I can't get to sleep when there's people running up and down the stairs.'

I felt that she is quite an isolated and fearful person and was prepared to show more of this side of herself.

SW	'Has anyone ever broken in?'	Reality testing.
Mrs E.	'No, but I don't like being on my own. I've blocked up the letter box and put a dresser in front of the back door. There was something going on last night when I turned on the TV. I could hear people's voices and footsteps outside. I went to bed but I couldn't get to sleep.'	She seemed to become quite anxious when talking about being alone.
SW	'In a block of flats like yours there are always lots of people around but it doesn't mean that they are going to do you any harm.'	Trying to reassure her.
Mrs E.	'What about the dosser sleeping in my outhouse?'	
SW	'What did you do about him?'	
Mrs E.	'I told him to go.'	
SW	'And did he?'	
Mrs E.	'Yes, he didn't come back again.'	She seemed a bit more in touch with her own power.
SW	'Do you think Kevin would enjoy a camping weekend?'	
Mrs E.	'Yes, he'd love it, but I don't want to be on my own.'	This had a flavour of resentment.
SW	'You'll have to separate from him one day, you know.'	

Mrs E.	'I know, but he's just as bad – he won't sleep on his own. I've got a boyfriend and it's not that I want sex but I would like some privacy sometimes.'	I felt that this was an issue but it didn't seem appropriate to discuss sex at the club.
SW	'Why don't you talk to Kevin about it and ask him to sleep in his own room?'	We had talked about this before and I had got nowhere as she finds it difficult to listen to any concrete suggestions.
Mrs E.	'He won't – he just comes into my bed in the middle of the night.'	She didn't want to hear.
SW	'If you make it clear to him that you want to sleep on your own, and when he comes in in the night take him back to his own bed and stay with him until he gets to sleep again, he would stop doing it quite soon.'	I was determined to try and present it as a simple matter.
Mrs E.	'No, he wouldn't.'	Still not wanting to hear.
SW	'It's quite an effort for a child to wake himself up in the middle of the night and get out of bed, when he realizes that you were going to take him back all the time he would give up.'	
Mrs E.	'He wouldn't, he does what he likes.'	This is quite a distorted view of K. in my opinion. It is Mrs E. who doesn't really want him to sleep on his own.

SW   'You will have to stop   I felt obliged to say this
          having him in your bed at   although I didn't think
          night soon, you know. He's she would respond.
          nearly 8 now and should be
          sleeping on his own.'

Mrs E.   'I know, but I can't stop   Still sticking to a percep-
          him.'   tion of herself as
                                      powerless.

SW   'The camping weekend may   She obviously had ambi-
          be a good chance to try out a valent feelings about the
          small separation, you may   camping weekend as she
          both cope with it better than had already said that K.
          you think. You would get   would like it. I thought
          the chance to spend time   she might be able to
          with your boyfriend and   respond to K.'s fears
          Kevin would realize that   more easily than her
          nothing terrible happens if own.
          he is not with you at night.'

Mrs E.   'I would like him to go. I She did respond this time.
          wonder how much it is.'

SW   'When I spoke to the man
          who organizes the club he
          said that they had special
          rates for people who are on
          social security. We can
          easily find out.'

Mrs E.   'It's really nice here, isn't it? This was the first time I
          Look at him, he's loving it.' had seen her expressing
                                      fondness for K.

SW   'Yes. He mixes very well   Encouraging her good
          with other children, doesn't feelings for K.
          he?'

Mrs E.   'Oh yes, there's a kid there K. was talking to a girl.
          that he knows from school.

	He loves running about and playing games. His school says that he's brilliant at sports.'	This was said with pride.
SW	'He seems to be doing well in the games here. He can run really fast, can't he?'	Again encouraging her feelings of pride.
Mrs E.	'He used to go to the Boy's Brigade but he won't go any more.'	I think he stopped going because she didn't support him.
SW	'Why is that?'	
Mrs E.	'I don't know, he just stopped going.'	
SW	'Perhaps he'll start going again in the summer – do any of his friends go?'	Having pushed her on the issue of sleeping arrangements I didn't want to risk any more conflict.
Mrs E.	'No – I don't think so.'	
SW	'What about the child he knows here, does she live near you?'	Hoping he might be able to go to the club with her.
Mrs E.	'I don't know – I've seen her around but I don't know where she lives.'	Not very interested.
SW	'If he does want to go to the Boys' Brigade again, the volunteer might be able to take him.'	Decided after all to try the Boys' Brigade idea again.
Mrs E.	'He went swimming with my friend on Saturday and he loved it.'	

We chatted for a bit longer and then Mrs E. said that she thought K. was OK. I asked her to go and tell K. that we were leaving and make sure that he felt OK. She did this and we left. On the way home I arranged to take the volunteer to meet her and K. the following week.

Analysis

I was very pleased and relieved that Mrs. E. kept the appointment and was ready to leave when I got there, as I felt that she was making it clear that she had changed her attitude towards me. She was much more relaxed and friendly than she had been in the past and was able to show the vulnerable part of herself to me. It was also the first time that she had shown her pride in K. as well as her dependence upon him. I think that it is very necessary that she starts to separate from him but it needs to be done carefully so as not to distress him. At the moment she seems not to have any idea as to how to begin to do this and will need help and support. She has ambivalent feelings about trying to separate a bit from K. as he compensates for the lack of close friends, particularly male friends. She does have a relationship with a man but it seems to be rather precarious as he lives with someone else. She tends to talk about him as a source of money but this is likely to be a defence against being hurt by him. I didn't pick up on the issue of sex because it didn't feel like an appropriate place to discuss it, but I felt that it was an issue for her. I think it would be good to try and involve Mrs E. in some sort of activity or part-time job as at the moment her only source of contact with the outside world is her local pub. When she is not feeling threatened she has a pleasant personality and is a sensible and caring woman.

End of the account written by the social worker.

DISCUSSION

This is a very different account. It offers an experience. The worker finds a way to recreate the immediacy of her perception of her client and of her experience of the client, and to make it clear that such experience is the pivot of her work. She finds some way of offering to the reader, to the critic, a sense of her own detailed understanding and response. Without each of the elements of criticism – experience, picture and analysis – no adequate evaluation can be made. This account offers an experience which is sharp and vital, realistic and alive. It offers detailed access to vivid communication, and a distinct complexity and coherence. It offers a style of description which seems complementary to the account of Ms Kennedy.

The task is to evaluate social work practice. It is possible to make some evaluation of this work because we know something of its vitality and its detail. Consider this short passage which marks Mrs Ellis's change of mood in the first interview.

> Mrs E.: It was selfish – I didn't think of leaving a note. (I knew I got through to her.)
>
> SW: Did you forget I was coming? (More gently.)
>
> Mrs E.: No, but it never crossed my mind to leave a note. You can't, here, anyway, someone might break in. (This sounded genuine and clear.)
>
> SW: All right – do you want Kevin to go to the club and to go out with the volunteer? (I was saying I had stopped fighting with her.)

This passage makes very clear the way in which social work is necessarily a matter of accurate intuition, of uncommonly reliable common sense. There is here no technology or esoteric knowledge, and yet this passage is one of the pivots of these two meetings. It is by such exchanges, and ultimately only by such exchanges, that the worker succeeds in offering help to her client. The passage shows the way in which the very essence of social work is the structure and use of communication and so, because this necessarily requires the worker to be immediately responsive, the way in which the worker must live the purpose of her work. Good social work is seen to be a matter of good intuition.

The passage records an 'ordinary' conversation, but it is clearly not ordinary in the way in which the worker shows that she retains a very clear, articulated purpose and a very exact sense of the way in which that purpose hinges upon meaning and the interpretation of meaning. She sees that the first phrase ('It was selfish') denotes a change of attitude, and tries both to acknowledge and to use this in her reply; she considers that this helps achieve a further change in her client's position and one which is sufficiently secure ('This sounded genuine and clear') to allow a shift in focus to more concrete and shared tasks ('Do you want Kevin to go to the club .... I was saying I had stopped fighting'). And from this shift develops the positive tone of the interview's conclusion and all the different avenues that are made accessible in the visit to the club.

The exchange is professionally purposeful – it seems that the worker could spell out both where she is going and why she plans to go there. Her account makes it possible to make some assessment of the exchange and to know something of how it was realized. But, although the account shows intent and an evident self-consciousness, it is clearly impossible for the worker to have contrived this exchange and to have made up her part within it. The discussion is necessarily a 'genuine' conversation – effective because of the immediacy of the worker's response, the integrity of her own feeling, the prompt subtlety of her understanding. In other words, her responses are spontaneous and thus a matter of intuition. It is possible for the worker subsequently to reconstruct her understanding, but at the time it can only have been a matter of 'just knowing' and 'just doing'. Understanding and action are therefore both intuitive and yet also fashioned exactly and delicately upon the worker's goal. Intuition is the vehicle by which the goal is realized; evaluation is a matter of assessing the quality of intuition.

The emphasis in the account of work with Mrs Ellis is always upon specific events and upon experience. Indeed, it seems to seek not to describe but to present events. It will be evident that there are costs in such an approach; as a complement to the earlier account, its strength and weakness are in complementary relation to those of that account. The strengths, though, are considerable, and offer the basis for a criticism, because they offer an experience upon which to base analysis. From this account it is possible to know in detail something of the real nature of the client, of the worker's experience of the client and of the process of her work with the client.

Is it plausible to claim that this account is 'real'? It is not a claim that is open to a certain kind of verification; there are no clear measures and no report of any independent observation. But it is a real account in the life-like manner in which the client is presented. We know from our experience, our intuition, that people *can* be like this and so the account assumes one kind of veracity which is not possible in more abstract descriptions. In this account the worker communicates a human experience – always the centre point for social work – with both coherence and complexity, and thus at least offers a possible basis for abstraction.

The reality of the account of Mrs Ellis given by the social worker lies in its rich, evocative immediacy. This worker in fact gives much less general or biographical information than was given in the account of Ms Kennedy, and this is a significant omission which ultimately does limit the value of the account. But to report, for example, the client's 'I told you to wait for the lady, you little bleeder' does more than would a discussion of Mrs Ellis's responsibility in relationship with her son and the social worker. To report in this way exactly – and simply – presents the reader with the problem about responsibility which the worker faces. In the same way the worker reports her client's anger, her vulnerability about aloneness, her fears of physical danger, her warm pleasure in her son's achievement. This diversity has a reality, a coherence, because we are told something of how it is lived by one person; though we know less of the complexity of Mrs Ellis's life, we do know how the available complexity is realized. The client, and her problems, are presented in something like the form in which we might expect to meet them. This is a manner of presentation which itself demonstrates a considerable creative capacity in the worker.

The worker describes her own experience with this same immediacy, indeed with more immediacy, because we can evaluate not only her words but her thoughts and observations. The manner in which she presents her work makes clear the sensitivity and diversity which must be present in her own response, and the way in which that response is necessarily genuine and spontaneous. The quality of her own involvement is seen to be her most important contribution to her client; she cares, she is angry, she is striving to be honest. She bases many of her assessments upon her 'feelings' ('I felt that she is quite an isolated and fearful person', 'I felt that this was an issue but it didn't seem appropriate to discuss sex at the club'), but these 'feelings' are less matters of emotion alone than reports of an awareness, which is intelligibly both thought and feeling. She clearly uses her imagination ('as though they were both children'). Her response, in other words, leans heavily and necessarily upon her intuition.

However, it is the quality, not the existence, of intuition which will determine competence. Intuition is universal; the worker must have not just common sense, but uncommonly good common sense. The worker must be artist to communicate her understanding and critic to evaluate the meaning of her client's and her own understanding. It is evident that the worker is alert in these ways. She explicitly evaluates her client's meaning ('This is quite a distorted view'), she seeks to test her own comprehension ('A joke to check out if she felt OK about the row'), she communicates her understanding ('encouraging her feelings of pride'). And she accomplishes these tasks within the framework of a larger overt task which is itself purposeful – the visit to the youth club. Her account is therefore evidently both ordinary, akin to any purposeful social encounter, and extraordinary, because she accepts responsibility to be accountable for her part in this ordinary exchange and seeks to show that she has used it for her client's best advantage. Good art has been shown to be the skilled mastery of ordinary means of communication, and this is therefore an account of the worker's art. Her work is a matter of 'lived experience'; it is what she does and what she is.

It is, nonetheless, her work and it must therefore be subject to evaluation. This account makes it possible to make some assessment of the work because of the detail it gives about the experience of the client and the worker. This account, like the first, reports a limited change in the client. She meets the worker angrily, she comes to show more uncertainty and vulnerability, she shows her pride in her son and she considers steps which will give new stimulus to mother and son. The character of the account makes it clear that these changes did not happen haphazardly. They are not the incidental but the explicit focus of the worker's effort, and her responses monitor and meet these changes as they are realized. To a limited degree, at least, change is seen to be achieved in these sessions, and because the account is rich in detail about intuitive knowledge and intuitive behaviour, the change can be related to the efforts of the worker. Is it therefore possible to conclude that this is an account of successful social work?

This account is interesting and positive, but it too fails to offer a sufficient account of practice. The account, as a complement to the first report, has the complementary strengths. It makes very clear the imaginative engagement of the worker and the continuing vitality of her participation and in consequence makes clear the human detail which gives sense to problem and response. The work has evident coherence. It also has complexity, but it is a much less elaborate and explicit complexity than was the apparent aspiration of the author in the first account. The account has abundant vitality, but it lacks any properly developed context. The worker reports almost nothing of the client's biography and circumstance, almost nothing of the client's perception of her problems and almost nothing of her own analysis. She assumes but does not adequately explain the legitimacy – or even the nature – of the goals and priorities upon which she has decided. Her account thus gives little scope for any independent assessment of goals and priorities. What is it about this family's plight that makes this style of interview and club attendance the most appropriate path to follow? It may be that these means could be substantiated, but they are not substantiated. Without this kind of information it is impossible to evaluate the appropriateness of the worker's understanding and thus of her action. The weakness of this account is that it lives *only* in the immediacy of the narrative.

In contrast, the first account showed the worker explicitly aware of a range of potentially relevant influences upon her client's experience and striving to organize her efforts around substantiated objectives. She discusses her perception and understanding of the problems, she tries to explain them and the steps she takes to meet them. That account is flawed because it fails to give adequate place to intuition and experience, but the author is seeking to write a different kind of account. She aspires to an account which has a greater potential fullness. To realize that fullness, however, her account must have something of the art of the second, just as the second account needs something of the reported complexity of the account of Ms Kennedy. Neither account is sufficient and both preclude the possibility of full evaluation. Both imply that work was effective, yet neither allows real credit to be given for the worker's likely achievement. In different ways, each account is unsuccessful.

All practice, and thus all account of practice, implies the possibility and legitimacy of evaluation. Nonetheless, in one sense it might be thought unfair to make comparison between these two accounts, for it has not been a comparison of like with like. One account is clearly intended as a general overview of work completed, the other as a narrative of selected detail – a 'process record'. The authors, in some degree, set out with different intentions and write different accounts in consequence; each could prepare (and in fact has prepared) accounts in the other style. Not all summaries and not all process records are written in the forms of these two accounts. Good summaries and good process records may be written with a different structure or in an entirely different style. In one way, though, these accounts can be deemed typical, for it is not unusual that each type of account lacks so much of the content of the other. This is not a necessary condition. The first account could have included material with a more experiential, intuitive emphasis and the second account could have developed more fully the sections of introduction and analysis. Yet each author clearly thought it appropriate to write their account largely within the constraints of only one approach.

The priority in the critical sequence of picture, experience and then analysis makes it possible to give a more approving response to simply experiential than to simply abstract accounts, because abstraction without experience is nonsense. But in social work the dichotomy itself is nonsense, for in social work there can be no division between theory and practice, between the abstract and the concrete – each founders without the other. Yet these two accounts, in the mutual exclusiveness of their approaches, attest to the common acceptance within social work of just that nonsense. The accounts highlight the problem of describing and evaluating practice, and illustrate – despite the sensitivity, fluency and competence of their authors – the general cultural acceptance of the 'fatally wrong approach' already noted by Raymond Williams: that every kind of activity suffers if it is abstracted and separated. The test of an adequate account of social work will evidently be an exacting one. Social work needs some styles, some conventions, which will allow it to manage its creativity and its criticism as a proper unity.

SOCIAL WORK WITH A DISABLED WOMAN AND HER HUSBAND

THE ACCOUNT WRITTEN BY THE SOCIAL WORKER

Mrs Claire W. moved from Scotland to the London Borough where she now lives when she was 20. She was originally referred to the department seven years ago. Four years before, aged 22, she was diagnosed as having a wasting, debilitating disease of the bowel, Crohn's Disease, and in those four years this condition had caused her to become very infirm; she was considered for possible social services support. There was no further contact with social services for three years, when a senior social worker at the hospital that Mrs W. attended wrote requesting regular social work support for Mrs W. Her letter stated that Mrs W. was still able to work part-time due to the kindness of her company. However, there was concern that Mrs W. was neglecting to care for herself and her house, and an indication that this may have a detrimental effect on her marriage. A social worker was allocated to Mrs W. two months later, and continued to visit for two years until she left the department, when the case was made non-active. During this period Mrs W. was required to give up her job due to increasing handicaps. The social worker encouraged Mrs W. to attend a centre for handicapped people two days a week, and to become involved in the activities of a local society for the physically disabled. When the social worker left Mrs W. was committed to these activities and receiving a good deal of support from them.

Last September Mrs W.'s GP contacted the department because Mrs W. was seriously considering having a baby. The doctor was concerned about the implications should Mrs W. proceed with her plan, due to the fact that Mrs W. herself needs a great deal of care and attention. The problems and probable outcomes were discussed with the duty officer, including the ultimate one of reception into care. It was agreed that Mrs W. may need skilled counselling in this matter, and the doctor planned to seek the advice of Mrs W.'s specialist.

The next contact with the department was made six weeks later. The GP phoned to express concern about the present family situation. The GP said that a 13-year-old girl had been visiting the home regularly at Mr W.'s invitation to do odd jobs, but had also sometimes been staying in the house overnight. Mrs W. was always present and there was no suggestion of any improper behaviour. However, Mrs W. was due to go into hospital for a fortnight's rest, and the GP expressed anxiety about what might happen if Mr W. got into trouble over the girl, and subsequently could not look after his wife.

During the period that Mrs W. was in hospital in November a formal referral was received from the senior social worker at the hospital. The letter stated that the 13-year-old girl, Vicky, was not attending school, was in trouble with the police for stealing, and was being seen by the child guidance clinic. It was also possible that she had a crush on Mr W. who himself was glad to have the company of someone who was not disabled. Mrs W. would be grateful for guidance and support from a social worker.

In reply, a month later, the senior social worker at the hospital was told that a social worker would visit Mr and Mrs W. in January. Part of the delay was due to the need to establish liaison with the child guidance clinic, as it was felt that the letter contained two separate referrals. In the report on file, it was recorded that Vicky's involvement with Mr and Mrs W. was unknown to the clinic, and it was felt by the psychiatrist that if the subject was raised, Vicky's father, a violent man, might react angrily against the clinic. The psychiatrist felt that social services should inform Vicky's parents of the connection. It was recorded that the first step would be to allocate a social worker to Mr and Mrs W. to 'find out from them what they said was going on'.

At my arrival in the agency in January this case was allocated to me. It was intended that after my initial visit it would be decided what action should be taken about Vicky. I was clearly instructed to restrict my involvement and concern to Mr and Mrs W., but at the same time to have my antennae out for information about Vicky, and to report back.

In retrospect it is clear that I should have used my antennae to clarify the position about inter-agency politics. The role of the child guidance clinic was unclear. It is still unclear, and I have not questioned the various manoeuvrings that took place, as they are not now relevant to the case. However, what is clear is that I felt at the time unable to question the basis on which the case was allocated, due to the fact that it was allocated on my first day in the agency. Agencies may generally expect newcomers to question the status quo, but probably not on the very first day.

I set about preparing for the interview. First came the file. Two aspects in particular caught my attention. First, much discussion of a personal nature about Mrs W. had been done without her knowledge. Her mother had been in to the office on several occasions to express anxieties while making it clear she did not want her daughter to be aware of the fact. Also, Mrs W.'s employers had made a complaint about her constant diarrhoea without the complaint reaching Mrs W., and subsequently discussed the termination of her employment with the social worker long before this event occurred. I speculated about this. Was this reluctance to talk frankly to Mrs W. due to her own difficulties in accepting her disabilities, or a function of other people's embarrassment? Was Mrs W. the victim of people who wanted to control her life, or had she a passive personality, and was pleased to relinquish control? Was it a function of the way she had coped with the problems of disability?

The second issue to emerge from the case notes gave some clues to this question, and had to do with the marital relationship. It was clear that Mrs W. had been a very attractive woman when she married, but her disabilities had taken their toll. It was recorded that Mr W. had complained that his wife was paying little attention to herself, and had said 'Look at that, who would fancy that?' pointing to his wife. Mrs W. had quietly agreed with him. It was clear that sexual relations had been disrupted, and the couple had been advised to seek help from an organization with experience of the sexual problems of the disabled. There were various references in the notes to Mr W.'s desire to have children, and the fact that a pet had taken the place of children. There were also references to Mr W.'s annoyance about having to cook for himself, and on one occasion he had requested help with the cooking and house cleaning. These points seemed to indicate that Mrs W. had not been given a chance to come to terms with her disability. The illness had been diagnosed after she was married, at the age of 22. The course of the disease meant she suffered a loss of her role as a wife in the traditional sense, and also her image as a woman. The notes indicated that Mr W. served as a constant reminder of these facts, and also that he found it difficult to adjust to the realities of his wife's disease. Rather than re-negotiating the basis of the relationship, it appeared that Mr W. was continuing to regard his wife in terms of what she could not give him. This could mean that Mrs W. was suffering from feelings of guilt, frustration, inadequacy and loss of self-esteem. If this was the case it could be the reason why people were reluctant to talk frankly to her, for fear of compounding these feelings in her.

Apart from orienting myself for the interview by reading the file, I re-acquainted myself with some facts about the disease. I was fairly familiar with it from nursing experience and I knew what sort of disabilities Mrs W. might have.

The first interview with Mrs W. was also my first interview in the agency. This was significant to me because it was to be the first time I would be representing a social services department as a social worker. I had for a long time aspired to be in this position, and naturally I wanted to get it right. I wanted to show the humane, caring side of the department, and not the bureaucrat-ized, time-pressured side. This is why, when I met Mrs W., I apologized for the length of time it had taken before she had seen a social worker. Mrs W. responded with a gesture that indicated she did have feelings about this. My internal response was to try and compensate for this by my approach. I wanted to indicate that I had plenty of time, and that I cared.

The first interview went something like this. Claire began by expressing concern about Vicky; how she was out of school, in trouble with the police and always round at the W.'s house. Claire and Brian felt they had done all they could to help her. They had tried and failed. I picked up what Claire had told me about herself and her husband, and she confessed that the real problem was that Vicky had a crush on Brian, and Brian couldn't see what was going on. Brian did nothing to stop Vicky's attentions, and even took her side against Claire, when Vicky was rude to Claire. Claire was feeling jealous, hurt and powerless to do anything. She wanted a man to talk to Brian. She also felt that Vicky was a substitute for a child of their own, as Brian had always wanted a child. At the end of the interview I agreed to visit Claire and Brian together, the next week.

As I left the house I felt very sad for Claire. She had extensive disabilities and was confined to lying on the sofa. She was very weak and clearly in great pain, and even preparing a cup of tea was a major task for her. As a person she appeared to be making a great effort to control her emotions. She talked steadily, ration-ally and also very carefully, and gave me very clear messages about how far to tread. If I ventured over a certain line, she told me to stop. For instance, at one point I suggested she might be worried about 'how far Brian might go with Vicky'. Claire immediately replied 'No'. She said that Brian would never do anything like that, but she is worried that Vicky, being the type of girl she is, might accuse Brian of going too far. He might get into trouble because no one could verify that he hadn't. Claire did not want to admit to the idea that Brian found Vicky sexually attractive. She did admit to feeling hurt that Brian allowed Vicky to flaunt herself in front of them both. He had allowed her to sit on his knee, and Claire had been obliged to mention this. It was as if Vicky was saying to Claire, 'Look what I can do with your husband.' However, Claire explained her hurt by saying that she was hurt that Brian could not see what was going on. What he really wanted was a child, and she would try and give him one.

I felt sad because Claire is a brave and capable woman. She was also clearly intelligent, thinking and someone who cares deeply for other people. Her disabilities meant that it was this part of her that needed to be stimulated and exercised, but her husband and the young girl seemed to be ignoring these aspects and instead punishing her with ideals of femininity and wifehood. I felt that Claire was fully aware that I saw through the transparencies of her defences, but I felt it was her way of communicating to me that I had to be very careful with her. Every day she was faced with the brutal fact that she was not attractive to her husband, and she couldn't fulfil her wifely functions as he would like her to. Her rational defences that 'Brian wouldn't do a thing like that', and 'I can cope with a baby, I'll find a way', were the only way of staving off an emotional crisis. And if she couldn't cope emotionally, on top of being grossly physically incapacitated, what would she have left?

The next week, events began to snowball. I received a phone call from a very irate GP. She couldn't understand why we weren't doing anything about Vicky. We had to get her out of the house. Claire's health had been deteriorating since she had been visiting. I suggested we meet to talk about it, and she arranged an immediate appointment. When we met she said that social services had to do something about Vicky. She thought it was unlikely that Brian had not had sex with her. One day the GP had seen upstairs and found some of Vicky's underclothes in Brian's room. The doctor also said that it was out of the question that Claire could cope with a baby: she wouldn't even be able to hold a newborn baby. I agreed to discuss the situation with the team leader, and to contact the doctor again. The team leader was out at the time, so I left a memo, and thought no more about it. My responsibility was to Claire, while the team leader still had responsibility for Vicky. I assumed the memo would cause immediate allocation of Vicky's case, and I also assumed I would confront Brian with the information at our interview. However, next the social worker who had been nominated to take the case if necessary asked me about the situation, and when I had outlined the GP's story she said we must speak to the duty team leader. They both agreed that the police should be informed immediately.

I phoned the GP to inform her what would happen. She said she wanted the police to keep her name out of it all. She felt that if Claire knew what she had done it would destroy the relationship. Next, the social worker for Vicky was asked to phone the police; I felt unable to do it. The police said they would call on Vicky the next day, and also Mr and Mrs W. They also wanted to speak to the doctor. I phoned her back, and she said she would phone them. She also said that her practice nurse had just told her that Brian had threatened to leave Claire if she turned Vicky out of the house. The doctor also told me in passing that her own marriage had just broken up.

I had the entire weekend to contemplate events. I was horrified at the implications of the situation. Whether Brian was charged or not it was possible that he would leave, and Claire would be bereft. I was caught in the classic social work dilemma of choice between accountability to my client, or to my agency and the state. An article by Pearson in Jones' (1975) book, *Towards a New Social Work*, succinctly explains the situation. Pearson says that social work values of confidentiality, client self-determination, non-judgemental attitude, acceptance and individuation are all explicit. These are the values on which casework rests. There is also an assumption that these values offer the client a limitless relationship. However, it is quite clear that 'the social worker is able to offer no such thing. For the social worker is an official of a bureaucratic organization as well as a person engaged in a "relationship"' (p. 51). While the rules of the relationship are explicit, Pearson suggests that the rules governing accountability to the organization are hidden. He outlines what these hidden rules might be.

(1) The client's communications to officials of a public service, involving as they do matters of public money, and in the last analysis, public order, have the character of public knowledge.
(2) The client's actions, impinging on the rights of others and on the obligations and priorities of public service, are not free.
(3) The client's actions, by their nature problematic to consensus, are judged.
(4) The client's rights as citizen do not entitle him to anticipate that regardless of any act on his part he will continue to be 'accepted': he can, in short, be outlawed.
(5) Clients, as the objects of large scale organizations with many bureaucratic features, will be treated within the administrative machinery as cyphers. (p. 53)

It is not surprising, then, to find Carl Rogers quoted as saying that 'Therapy and authority cannot be co-existent in the same relationship' (p. 64). The two sets of rules completely cancel each other out. The social worker's value system becomes empty in situations where a person's position towards law and order come into conflict with the client/social worker relationship. As Plant says, 'caseworkers need, but do not possess, an adequate moral and social theory' (Plant, 1970, p. 6).

What happens to the social worker in these situations? In my case I was left feeling guilty. Guilty for possibly exposing Claire to the danger of the collapse of her world, and guilty because in the first instance it had not occurred to me that I had a duty to phone the police with the information the doctor had given me. And additionally I felt angry that I had discarded my traditional social work values; I suppose I felt I had been compromised.

The literature relating to values and ethics in social work invariably states loud and clear that the only way through the mirky quagmire is to think clearly, and to ask questions. Pearson says 'unless the profession of social work faces its moral and political ambiguities squarely, there can be little hope of transcending the professional uncertainty of the worker' (Jones, 1975, p. 66). Bruce Hugman talks about a need to question and challenge, and to maintain 'energetic vigilance with regard to what one is told to do, expected to do, what one imagines one is supposed to do and the reality or fantasy of authority which lies behind such things. It relates also to the large questions about what the agencies' purposes are' (Brake and Bailey, 1980, p. 135). And Day concludes his book on *Social Work and Social Control* by saying: 'If there is self-deception and lack of integrity towards others then the social work enterprise becomes intellectually disgusting and morally and politically reprehensible: with greater openness, healthy debate, and compromise the potential strength of consensus is realized' (1981, p. 229).

To return to the case, I have now learned, through my mistakes, that it is imperative to keep objectives and values explicit. It should have been clear that there was the potential for a clash of values in this case. Concern for Claire and concern for Vicky were mutually exclusive, but I was obliged to become involved with Vicky, and her welfare. The first thing I should have done is question why Vicky's case had not been allocated. Secondly, I found myself swept along with the decision to phone the police. As Hugman points out, new staff are very rapidly socialized to agency norms (Brake and Bailey, 1980, p. 132), and it was easy for me to blame myself for not realizing that I had a duty to society and the agency. However, had I questioned what was happening the issues involved would have been clearer. It was implicit in the decision that the agency was concerned that there was a risk that Vicky was in 'moral danger'. Brearley, in his book on *Risk and Social Work*, (1982), states clearly that a thorough analysis of situations is needed to deal effectively with risk. One must be aware of the events that are available as options, know the relative importance of each outcome to the client, and include in evaluation the gravity and imminence of outcomes. What happened in this case was that we acted on the statement of the doctor that it was unlikely that sex had not occurred. However, no one had met Brian or Vicky, and the information from the doctor was given when she was very angry and wanted something done to protect Vicky. We also discovered too late that her own marriage had just broken up, and it is possible that this also affected her feelings about Claire's situation. Additionally, we did not consider what the probable outcomes of any course of action might be. We did not know whether Brian would be charged with an offence, and we did not know how Claire might respond. We did not know if the information given was likely to be true. The decision to phone the police was made because (1) the doctor's statement was treated as reliable, and because (2) the agency needed to protect itself against accusations of irresponsibility.

Brearley states that 'we cannot precisely identify the acceptability of risks if we cannot first describe and analyse the risks themselves' (1982, p. 61). He then goes on to describe risk in terms of hazards, dangers and strengths. Only having done this can one balance probabilities and evaluations of outcomes. In this case all hazards, dangers and strengths were not considered; only the set which related to Vicky, and even then only cursorily. I made a mistake in not questioning the way in which the decision was made. I accepted the hidden rules of the establishment and so laid myself open to the moral crisis I experienced.

By the next week it was clear that the police had not yet acted, so I went ahead with the interview with Brian and Claire as planned. The purpose was to hear Brian's own account of the situation, and to see how far he was aware of the effect of his behaviour on Claire. I was not intending to act as an advocate for Claire or relinquish my impartiality. Brian began by being very defensive. He said he didn't know what all the fuss was about, felt they had a duty not to turn Vicky out of the house as it would hurt her feelings, and said he felt Claire was jealously over-reacting. He regarded Vicky in the same way he would a daughter. Claire reacted to this by reiterating that Vicky is growing up, becoming sexually aware, and although he regarded her as a daughter, she felt it was clear that Vicky had a crush on Brian. Claire wanted Vicky not to visit any more. As time went on, and I maintained an impartial and clarifying role, Brian began to state his point of view more explicitly. He said that he had always wanted children, and he enjoyed Vicky's company. He felt that Claire's illness had deprived him of fatherhood, and that now he had a right to enjoy children's company. He felt that Claire was jealously mistrusting him and he wanted her to have faith in his integrity. He saw it as a test of the marriage. Claire in her turn began to express feelings of hurt, and said that if she wasn't ill she would go and find a boyfriend for herself.

I came away feeling that Brian and Claire were treading very carefully with each other's feelings. While both had agreed they had set tests for their partner – Claire testing Brian's love for her, and her alone, and Brian testing Claire's trust in him – neither admitted the underlying feelings, which if admitted could result in divorce. Brian would not admit that he fancied Vicky and not Claire, and Claire did not admit the extent of her hurt. They seemed to have reached a precarious stalemate.

The next day the police questioned Vicky. She admitted that she had sometimes partly undressed with Brian and Claire. Brian was questioned and the police decided that there was no offence and no charge would be made. He was cautioned about showing inappropriate interest in girls under the age of 16. There was never any question that Brian had had sex with Vicky, and Claire stated that she had on all occasions been present when Vicky had undressed. Claire and Brian were not told who had informed the police. They believed it to have been an acquaintance of Vicky.

The following week when I visited Claire and Brian talked about the police visit. I used the opportunity to talk about how they both felt about the possibility of a charge, and how they felt about each other. Brian restated his stance about wanting Claire to trust him, and Claire talked about the emotional effect this had on her. She indicated that she didn't know how long she could withstand the trauma of conceding to her husband's demands, and Brian indicated he would leave her if she did not. At the end of the interview Claire and Brian both said they did not want any more joint interviews, and Claire wanted to see me on her own.

Having agreed to this I wondered if it was the right thing to have done. First, I was implicitly colluding with Brian, and acknowledging that Claire was the weaker party. Secondly, I had seen some movement away from the rational defences that they were both putting forward, and if I persevered it was possible that Claire and Brian could strengthen their marriage by reassessing their contracts with each other. On the other hand, such an approach could lead to a separation, and in any case, what right had I to impose my regime of casework on these two people? What right had I to interfere with their private contracts, however unbalanced I felt them to be?

The question has to do with the thorny topic of self-determination. There has been much debate about the issue, centring round the problem of what actually is this thing called self-determination if a social worker constantly limits the capacity because of constraints of reality. Biestek states that 'the client's right to self-determination is limited by the client's capacity for positive and constructive decision making, by the framework of civil and moral law and by the function of the agency' (Plant, 1970 p. 26). There is not scope in this essay to discuss the implications of this statement in terms of the client, for in this case the issue has more to do with the rights of a social worker to determine how to proceed with casework. If there are real constraints on a client's rights, so also are there the same constraints on the rights of a social worker. I felt that Claire was allowing herself to be subjected by her husband, and wanted her to be free from those constraints in order for the relationship to exist on a more equal emotional basis. However, if I pursued this ideal on behalf of Claire I would be ignoring the reality of her disability. A danger of the pursuit of this ideal might be the break up of the marriage, and yet Claire was dependent on Brian to a large extent. In practical terms, how would she manage without him? Just as the client's rights to self-determination are limited by the constraints of reality, so the social worker's rights to work towards freedom from constraints are also limited by reality.

At my next interview with Claire we discussed why they had decided not to pursue joint interviews. Claire said that they felt it was too dangerous. They had begun to express their feelings about their present situation, and both found themselves saying things they hadn't meant to say. The logical conclusion of some of these things was divorce, which Claire didn't want. She felt that if she could express her feelings of hurt, pain and anger to me, she could survive the contract she and Brian had made between them. The only way it would work was if she 'kept her head'. I suggested that she might also look for ways of decreasing her dependance on Brian and she agreed to this. So the purpose of my visits was to help Claire express her feelings, to support her efforts to maintain a rational balance in her relationship with Brian, and to explore ways of increasing her self-esteem by lowering her dependence on Brian.

Claire used the first few interviews to express her feelings about Brian. She confessed that she couldn't be upset in front of him as he saw it as a sign of weakness. She had cried once, and he had hit her. One of the dominant feelings expressed was anger. Claire soon connected this feeling to her frustration about the constraints of her disability. If she were well she would never lie back and accept Brian's behaviour, she would fight it. She compared herself to her father who died four years ago, saying that he had always been known as a 'bonnie fighter'. She was really a bonnie fighter underneath, but couldn't demonstrate it. On several occasions Claire indicated she might call a solicitor to instigate divorce proceedings in order to shock Brian. She wanted to do something to show she was fighting him, and not meekly accepting his demands. During these interviews I encouraged Claire to talk about her feelings, and also consistently encouraged her to recognize her considerable strengths. I pointed out her ability to think clearly, her determination to cope emotionally and her considerable capacity to continue to support Vicky as she began a new school, despite her anger towards her. Very quickly Claire was rediscovering her capacity to transcend wallowing in her emotions, and to use them to act thoughtfully instead.

After a month Claire was once again very depressed, and feeling unable to cope. We explored why she felt this way, and she related it to a feeling of frustration. She had collapsed in the kitchen the day before, and said that when her physical limitations became so apparent she feels less able to cope with all the other pressures of her situation. It was the week after this that Claire told me that she had decided to go to a homeopath. She had made an appointment, and was very optimistic about it helping her. She talked about one day being able to walk again.

The issue of homeopathy touches on my own assumptions about physical disease. While there is little known about the causes of Claire's disease, there have been connections made between it and the immune system. It is well known amongst researchers into psychosomatic medicine that diseases relating to auto-immunity have psychosomatic associations. In this connection, I remember pricking my ears up when Claire said that because the illness had been diagnosed four months after her marriage, she had commented at the time that she must be allergic to Brian. Just as it is well known that social and psychological factors can cause disease, it is also well known that there are social and psychological factors which affect various cures. The placebo response is an example of this, and there are hundreds of examples of miraculous cures, and highly dubious treatments which have resulted in healing. Totman (1979) postulates that the psychological mechanism at work in these cases is one of cognitive dissonance. Festinger's theory of cognitive dissonance broadly states that after a person has made a decision, he will justify it, and the more difficult the decision, the greater the need there is to concoct reasons for choosing it. Thus, if a person subjects himself to a medical procedure which is difficult — expensive, painful or disreputable — the best justification for undergoing it is the fact of a cure: 'I'm glad I did it because now I'm better.' The act of justification activates the person's unconscious into affecting the treatment.

It was on the basis of this theory, and not a vague notion of the wonders of alternative medicine about which we as yet know very little, that I supported Claire's decision to go for homeopathic treatment. She had decided that the best way to help herself was to attack her disease. When she was better she would have more options open to her about how to respond to Brian. She would submit to the need to hide her feelings and keep her head as long as she was laid out, immobile on the sofa. When she became mobile she would fight. In fact, after only a short period of treatment, Claire began to move more easily, and this progress has been maintained. The treatment seems expensive and she dare not tell her GP what she is doing. However, it is still worth it.

Since that time Claire has become far more confident and assertive. There have been two occasions when she has been blatantly patronized because of her disease, both relating to an idea that she should not be told or bothered with family problems because she mustn't be worried. She responded with indignation, and then proceeded to become involved in the family problems and help resolve them. Claire no longer talks about how to cope with Vicky, as she knows she copes very well with her. She is confident in her ability to help her. Neither does she express a longing to have a baby. She is looking after herself first, and seeing this as her first priority.

While theories and constructions about people can be documented, it is difficult to convey an important part of the social work process, that of the style of the worker. During the joint interviews with Brian and Claire, it was important to maintain an independent role, and to seek to clarify their respective positions. The decision not to continue with these interviews was made because both felt it was too dangerous to get so close to complete honesty and candour. Having decided that Claire would, in effect, be the one to back down to save the marriage, my role was to help Claire to maintain her own sense of integrity. I listened to her a great deal, and tried to help her clarify why she was doing what she was doing. I maintained a position of great respect for Claire's considerable strengths and tried to renew her confidence in herself. At the last interview to date Claire said that she had a new hold on herself, and that she felt she had been in danger of giving in to her disease, and to other people's expectations that there was little she could do.

End of the account written by the social worker (References cited in the account are included in the general list of references at the end of the book.)

DISCUSSION

This is a rich account which offers considerable possibilities for discussion and which does make possible an evaluation of the worker's practice. It also makes possible the discussion of a number of broader issues, some of them explicitly acknowledged – for example, moral issues of worker and agency role and issues about worker 'style' – and some of them implicitly acknowledged, for example, the worker's use of theory in her practice. It will therefore be relevant to consider not only the quality of the social work practice described in the account, but also those qualities in the account itself which make the account so useful.

This account tells a story, as should all good reports of social work. The story is partly a tale about a client, partly a tale about the worker. A part of the value of the account, as will be seen, lies in the relative emphasis given to these different foci. In the beginning of the story Claire is dependent and unhappy, at the end she appears to be slightly less dependent and slightly less unhappy, and this change seems to be sensibly linked to the events described by the worker, including the efforts and activities of the worker herself. The causes of the change are no more empirically verifiable than in the previous accounts, but to assert the link in this situation seems plausible when judged by common sense and common experience. Claire changes because she comes to experience the world in a somewhat different way. She becomes clearer about certain of her immense difficulties and adopts a more active stance in relation to them; instead of hiding from problems by staying (literally) immobile, she is able to see and reach for possibilities that may realistically give her a greater mastery and independence. The quality of the social work lies in the formulation and realization of these possibilities.

Claire's progress is marked by stages which can be readily understood within the client-centred model of helping; the worker consistently strives to understand the client's detailed experience and so to help the client clarify, accept and then act upon this experience. There can be no other basis for action, for social work *is* a 'client-centred' – or 'person-centred' – activity and no other procedure except such detailed and sensitive understanding of the person can offer the chance of effective work. This is true even though social work is not a 'clincial' encounter. It is social work's strength, and its challenge, that it involves itself in the confusions that exist beyond the confines of a more detached helping relationship, as this account well witnesses. It requires of the worker, nonetheless, that same measure of other-centred and exact sensitivity. The difference is that the social worker works, as it were, with her sleeves rolled up.

The stages through which Claire progresses seem to be, first, her wish to have a child to fulfil the original aspirations of the marriage; secondly, an exploration (a brief one – perhaps too brief) of the conflicts and confusions that exist currently within the marriage, which lead her to conclude that she must distance herself in some measure from her husband; and, thirdly, a preliminary foray into the implications and possibilities of her position, a foray which leads not only to periods of obvious depression but also to a much more optimisitc self-assertion. Thus, at the end of the account the worker can report a change in Claire: some change in behaviour, and some in attitude which may lead to further behavioural change. The worker cannot obscure the formidable difficulties which remain but she has helped Claire make some distinct and positive steps. The worker has helped achieve a basis for the future which is, in some degree at least, more hopeful.

The worker helps effectively because of the accuracy with which she shares the meaning of the client. It is only this understanding which she offers, and it is only this understanding which helps her to negotiate the ambiguities of the agency's practice (the delay, the referral to the police) with which she is associated. The account makes clear that the worker's effort is consistently directed towards a detailed realization of the client's experience and that her work is effective because of the exactness of her understanding and her ability to communicate it to her client. Thus the worker is seen to begin, before her first meeting with Claire and her husband, by 'speculating' on the family's attitude to the disability, and in particular on the issues of dependence and of marriage. She also ensures that she is informed about the character of the disease. She cannot, at this stage, 'know' about these aspects of Claire's life, but she is evidently attempting to ensure that she is prepared to formulate specific issues with all the speed that is possible. In other words, the worker is preparing to be accurately intuitive. Indeed, she has already relied upon this intuition for, when reviewing the file, significant information 'catches her attention'; the significance of her previous (formal and informal) learning is yielded not by formula but by a personal response.

The report of the first interview shows the way in which an emphasis upon accurate empathy continues to demand an emphasis upon intuition. The worker 'picks up' Claire's concerns about her marriage (which Claire then 'confesses' – an unfortunate expression) and she then reports her sense of the discussion itself and the light it casts upon Claire's wider experience. Her efforts are consistently directed towards establishing a reconstruction of the way in which Claire must see the world, and this is an effort which can be effective only by the use of her own imaginative response. This quality of imagination informs her attention throughout the work. Claire is helped because the worker recognizes pain (e.g. Claire was 'jealous, hurt and powerless', she was faced daily 'with the brutal fact that she was not attractive to her husband') and because the worker understands hope (e.g. 'when she became mobile she would fight'); these are necessarily acts of imagination, and thus of intuition, and it is therefore this intuition which underpins all the worker's key decisions (e.g. to work with the marriage, to accept the decision not to work with the marriage) throughout her contact. The worker is effective because of her knowledge, but her knowledge knows as much of the significance of 'being a bonnie fighter' as it does of the researched significance of the disease. The worker's knowledge can be seen to rest upon the worker's intuition, and upon the sufficient accuracy of that intuition.

The perspective of the client-centred model makes clear that Claire is able to make constructive decisions at each stage because her experience has been realized, or made accessible, by communicating it to another person, to the worker. The worker is understanding, but she does still have 'her sleeves rolled up', as she wades through the confusions of statutory responsibilities, home visits, role conflicts, social networks and so on. She contrives accurately to grasp her client's meaning, and to do so in a way which comprehends enough of this diversity. She indicates something of the merit of social work, that it is in social work's willingness to share immediately in the diversity and confusion of the client's world that it negates absurdity and achieves something of grandeur.

Is this, then, grand social work? It is not, even though it has such evident merits. The worker's intuition is 'sufficiently accurate' because it comprehends enough of the realities of Claire's experience, but it is only 'sufficiently' accurate, because it is too much confined to Claire's particular realities. The worker's decisions about her priorities and focus are not fully reported and so it remains possible that Claire, Brian and Vicky might have been better served if the work had had some different emphasis. The worker reports plausibly enough her decision, and her doubts, as she ceases to conduct joint interviews with husband and wife, but that decision comes in the wake of a consistent focus upon Claire's experience, and not upon the experience of Brian and Vicky. This may have been an appropriate or a necessary priority, but in a situation which is so evidently a charged *social* situation, it is a loss that other actors have so little fullness and complexity. We cannot properly assess the work without a greater comprehension of the others involved within it. It is a merit of the account that it makes so vividly clear the need for an awareness of the influence of different actors (who include the worker's colleagues as well as her clients). It is in consequence an evident defect that the work is so uneven in its development of this awareness.

The worker is aware that much confusion in social work can be minimized if careful attention is given to the establishment of clear values and objectives. It is evident that she is considerably distressed by the confusion and (in her view) inappropriate behaviour which a lack of articulated agency values and objectives has imposed upon the client. But the worker's practice is in some measure flawed by these same omissions; her values and objectives are too frequently implicit, not explicit, and although her related thinking is often given in considerable and interesting detail, she in fact actually fails to spell out properly her intentions and her reasons for formulating them. To an extent her goals (like those of the two previous workers) remain obscured and her work lacks a certain clarity in consequence; it casts light enough to indicate the social complexity of the situation, but not enough to make fully clear the reasons for selecting the path she chooses through it.

But although it is possible to point to less developed aspects of this account, it is quite unnecessary to labour them. A 'sufficiently accurate' intuition implies a 'good enough' social work. The worker might (and only 'might') have helped her clients more, but it is clear nonetheless that she certainly did help Claire. The work would be better with a sense of Brian's (and Vicky's) needs, without the confused response to the agency's referral to the police, and with a clearer statement of intention, but Claire does change and this change is seen to be a product of the worker's effort. 'Good enough', after Bowlby, is a phrase with positive connotations for social workers. This work is good enough because the worker has an evidently positive effect. So this is an account of sufficiently successful social work.

It is important, then, if this account makes possible an evaluation of the quality of the worker's practice, that the account itself is evaluated to make clear the ways in which it allows such judgements to be made. This account offers access which permits evaluation of both understanding and action; it is possible from this account to assent to or dissent from the worker's stance because so much relevant information is given. It is an irony of many social work accounts that they *cannot* easily be challenged, because they contain assertions but offer no adequate substantiating detail. The first account, of Ms Kennedy, had something of this quality; it gave *only* statement. It offered a general profile, selected facts, and a distant narrative of the social worker's action. The statements did not lend themselves to confirmation because there was no way of rooting assertion to give assertion substance. The second account, in a quite different way, permitted of little greater assessment. It offered vivid detail which had credence because of its colour and fluency (qualities which should be highly valued in social work), but it gave insufficient account of the context of the client and the thinking of the worker.

No one style of account will come to represent social work, but genuinely effective accounts will have to fulfil both the conditions of the critic (the analysis of the first account) and of the artist (the evocation of the second). The virtue of the account of work with Claire is that it so deftly moves between the two; it encompasses – as social workers must – both the general and the particular. It achieves its effect because the worker is able both to evoke and to theorize. It immediately offers specific detail ('she was originally referred to the department') but also quickly makes it evident that it will be an independently minded account ('In retrospect it is clear that I should have used my antennae to clarify the position about inter-agency politics'). This duality is established at the outset when the worker reads the file notes in preparation for the interview. She straight away shows a faculty for identifying relevant detail (Eliot's 'a sense of fact') and for interpretation (beginning the search for Leavis's 'essential order'); she can both pick out events and give them some – possible – broader meaning, and she does both with a deft directness. The account acquires immediately the air of both factual complexity and orderly coherence, not abstract, but evidently (and necessarily) rooted in a human nature, or common human experience, to which we can ourselves refer.

The key to this 'common human experience' is that the account makes it possible to share an experience and it does this by presenting, not denying, the worker's own experience. The client is visible because the worker is visible; we can see the client because we can see her through the worker's eyes. The worker uses language such as 'the first interview went something like this', which reminds us that *she* is organizing the account. She makes clear her own response – 'I felt very sad for Claire ... I felt sad because Claire is a brave and capable women' – because *her* experience, clearly defined, helps us consider how we ourselves might have experienced Claire. She moves, in her report of that first interview, through three tiered paragraphs which progress from descriptive summary to interpretation, to show the achievement of her own understanding. And in this way she makes it clear that she can see the wood and the trees, and that the one is nonsense without the other.

The worker makes consistent use of a style which asserts her own presence, never egocentrically, but always as a means to make her client clearer; the worker grasps that she is the only possible route to this clarity. Her early questions – 'Was this reluctance to talk frankly . . .? Was Mrs W. the victim . . .?' – draw attention to the worker's thinking, but this helps to define the possible character of the client's situation. The worker explains her own beliefs with care – 'The issue . . . touches upon my own assumptions' – but only to explain her practice, which in turn throws light upon the client's change. The worker emphasizes her imagination – to write 'She was really a bonnie fighter underneath, but couldn't demonstrate it' does more than report Claire's own evocative image – it indicates that the worker accepts the image, and that she invites us to do so too. She makes it possible for us to accept the intimate currency of the image which, precisely because it is an image, with simplicity and directness constitutes an enormously effective description. Thus the strength of the account lies always not simply in its vital portrayal of the client's experience, but in the vitality of the portrayal of the social worker's relevant experience. It makes it clear that it is only through reporting her consciousness that the worker can give plausible life to her account of others. It makes it clear that to know of the worker's knowledge and action we must know of the worker herself.

The account also helps to make clear the way in which the worker's consciousness cannot be 'clinically' restricted to a knowledge only of her client. It may be a weakness of the practice that the worker gives her most vivid attention only to Claire, but it is a strength of the account that it shows that the worker cannot really confine her attention only to one person. A social work attitude is not a matter for the client, or even for clients, alone; the worker's understanding of colleagues and agency will be a crucial determinant of her effectiveness. Consider, for example, the worker's evaluation of the GP's judgement. The inappropriateness of the doctor's insistence upon action *might* have been recognized by giving heed to her report of her own matrimonial stress. Such a reference is necessary to explain the character and quality of the worker's judgements, but, just because it refers to a professional colleague, it makes it abundantly clear that the worker lives in a world in which the focus cannot be upon a single defined centre of consciousness – 'not any one ... but the many persons' – all of them potentially active and inter-active, positive and negative.

The account also makes unequivocally clear the importance of the worker's understanding and response to her own role. The client's capacity to cope, as a function of the interaction between her inner world and the world in which she lives, includes the worker and agency as features of her environment, and thus – in Pincus and Minahan's (1973) terms – the 'change agent system' may well also be a part of the 'target system'. The worker makes clear the significance of her role and the stress of working in liaison with, or under the direction of, colleagues whose interpretation of their role she may think incorrect or inadequate. This is experienced (as in some degree, social work must always be experienced) as an intimately personal matter ('I had the entire weekend to contemplate events. I was horrified') and as a personal responsibility ('I made a mistake in not questioning the way in which the decision was made. I ... laid myself open to the moral crisis ...'). She sees that it was her failure to clarify her role which meant that she could not adequately assert that role. But it is only because of her explicit discussion of this failure that she makes clear the importance of the role itself and the significance of her experience of the role. The discussion emphasizes yet again that accounts of social work are intelligible only as they take detailed and specific account of the social worker.

A pattern is established which makes clear the consistent importance of a proper report of the worker's 'use of self', of her use of intuition. It is a further virtue of this account that it makes clear the manner in which the social worker necessarily blurs intuition with the use of theory. It is evident that 'theory' is not constantly at the forefront of the worker's mind; she recounts her thinking – for example, about the preparation and conduct of the first interview – and although she formulates questions and makes assumptions, they are not seen as requiring scholarly legitimation. Her understanding has been previously extended by formal as well as informal learning, but at this stage it is all one aspect of her own response, her intuition. It is not intellectually problematic. Her understanding of her own and the agency's role, however, *is* problematic; she feels confused and in error, and needs to clarify the difficulty. It is at this point that she has to look to theoretical material which will help her to make sense of the problem, and she makes a retrospective selection of theory familiar to her (e.g. Pearson, Brearley) which will help order the confusion. This seems in the account a self-evident procedure. How else might people clarify difficulties? But it makes it very clear that social work does not, and cannot, operate by the systematic application of previously determined theory. The problem precedes the theory, and the social worker necessarily plunders her 'knowledge pile' to characterize the problematic reality. The test of validity can only be whether or not the theory helps to make sense of the one situation; it may or may not be material which helps in the next.

It is not important, in this respect, that I do not agree with the worker's apparent conclusions about a necessary antipathy between authority and helping. It is important that she enables me to get a clear understanding of her thinking, and thus to be in a position to evaluate it. The account makes clear that the integration of theory with theory, and the integration of theory with practice, is ultimately a unique process, specific to the occasion and to the worker's perception of that occasion. It is a matter of intuition. The worker is articulate about *her* problems and *her* thinking, citing the specific and selecting from the general, and it is because, and only because, of this articulation that it is possible to evaluate her analysis. This analysis – about role – is no different from the use of knowledge in any other aspects of social work; the worker uses theoretical knowledge not to apply formulae, but to *construct* coherence from immediate complexity.

This account permits the evaluation of social work practice because it makes the social worker sufficiently visible as a person in relation to her work. We know the client only because we see her through the worker's eyes. For the same reason we know something substantial about the worker's response to the client. At the end of the account the worker notes the importance of 'style' in social work practice. This is a concept which points to that same personal emphasis that lies within an idea of intuition. It points to the necessary importance of the personal and the subjective. The worker seems to suggest that this is not, in her view, a matter of mere idiosyncrasy, but a necessary part of social work which must be the explicit subject of report and exploration. It is not a matter, however, which is usually made so clearly accessible, and to achieve this access the worker writes the account itself in a particular style: neither report nor drama, but something of a narrative essay, mixing the forms of story and discussion. It is not the only possible style for good accounts of social work – indeed, it is one which many of us would find hard to master. But it does offer one model for the demonstration in social work of the integration of theory with practice, of the concrete with the abstract, of the elements which social work, and descriptions of social work, must include. This is the merit of this report; it gives an access to the reality of the worker's practice which few accounts of social work are capable of yielding.

PADDLING IN THE FOOTHILLS

When the phrase 'paddling in the foothills' came to mind as a description of this section my first reaction was to scorn my mixed metaphor. On reflection I decide to keep the phrase because it does in fact seem to convey the intended meaning. The comments in these pages have been mere critical paddling, splashings that do not attain even the height of the first small hills. But the conception that social work must take seriously the need for a rounded description and appraisal of practice, and do it in something like these terms, is a conception which has real substance. In that sense this chapter has been exploring the foothills, and by implication there will be bigger heights, and these will have to be scaled in their turn.

This chapter has been something of a cheat. I set out to evaluate social work practice after making bold the claim that social work is art, or art-like. Yet my comments have inevitably, given their context, been constrained by a wider concern to point to the very possibility of such evaluation and to discuss the nature of the conditions which would seem to make it possible. My comments have not been allowed the necessary 'complete responsiveness' but have had instead, in their own way, that same 'judicial, one-eye-on-the-standard approach' which, in an earlier chapter,

F. R. Leavis was seen to find incompatible with true realization. I have sought to note not only something of the intrinsic quality of each work, but also something of the means and form which gave access to that quality – a divided purpose, albeit a necessary one, and so one in which the real potential of such an approach cannot be realized. It will be important, however, if it has been glimpsed.

The limitations of my own comments are not the only possible objections to the pieces in this chapter. It is a common challenge to detailed 'records' of social work that they cannot be authentic because there is no guard against the worker's faulty memory and inventive imagination. The accounts may not therefore be 'the truth'. The counter to this objection is implicit in the concept of social work as art; indeed 'the truth' has already been encountered as T. S. Eliot's provisional description of the outcome of competent critical inquiry. There can be no truth independent of the worker's own experience and it is that experience which the worker must find adequate means of constructing. To evaluate social work it is necessary to rely upon the worker's 'sense of fact', upon the complexity and coherence of the account which is communicated. There is an inherent improbability, though not an impossibility, that a worker will create a soundly rounded, convincing, detailed account, which is itself quite wrong; the real likelihood is that bad work, because it has no inherent clarity which can be communicated, cannot yield a clear account (except an account which clarifies the sources of the work's failure). Apparent clarity, apparent authenticity, in an account of social work cannot be a guarantee of competence, but it is an indication of likely competence. It is not a measure which social work can afford to ignore.

It is a possible objection that this description is a circle, a tautology, and that the only good social workers are said to be those who can describe good social work. In some measure, this *is* what I am saying. Good social work requires of the worker an ability to be very aware about personal experience and to communicate that awareness, and these are the skills of the author of the good account. But the good worker need not be master of the formal form of the account, and need not achieve that *precise* definition which is in art. But something of the form must be possible and thus good social workers must have at least something of this same expressive ability. It is not a problem, however; good social workers *do* have this ability and show it repeatedly in the colour and imagination, the humour and vitality of their informal description. The task becomes to legitimate its expression within the formal professional routine.

It may not be necessary that each social worker be capable of the published form, but social workers will need the published form to guide their practice. These accounts constitute the mere foothills of the venture in more ways than one, for it is not only that social work must search for excellent accounts of social work, but it must find accounts which reflect the diversity of social work. The accounts used in this chapter have had a narrow focus. They are taken only from one kind of agency setting, they emphasize only a narrow range of the problems with which social workers are acquainted, and they each tend to focus upon direct work with just one client. Their very selection was compromised for they were chosen, from a much broader range, not because of their intrinisic worth alone but because of the scope they offered to further an argument. Accounts are needed which in fuller measure show the experience of social work, in different settings, with different problems, and with different degrees of success and failure. A 'literature' – in the imaginative meaning of the term – of social work must aspire not only to the quality of a literature but also to the diversity of a literature.

Moving up from the foothills will be a long business. It will also be a business which will help change the very texture of social work. To realize properly the meaning of social work as art does not rest solely, or even primarily, upon the creation of a social work literature, but it is one necessary strand in the creation of a genuinely substantial social work. A social work literature will play a significant part in future change. It will also mean that social workers can at last look forward to the possibility of a good read.

References

Abercrombie, M. L. J. (1969), *The Anatomy of Judgement* (Harmondsworth: Penguin).

Association of Teachers in Social Work Education (1980), 'CCETSW proposals on assessment guidelines: ATSWE's response', *ATSWE Newsletter*, no. 29, pp. 7–11.

Bartlett, Harriett (1970), *The Common Base of Social Work Practice* (New York: National Association of Social Workers).

Berger, John, and Mohr, Jean (1976), *A Fortunate Man: The Story of a Country Doctor* (London: Writers' and Readers' Cooperative).

Berger, Peter L., and Luckmann, Thomas (1967), *The Social Construction of Reality* (London: Allen Lane).

Biestek, F. (1957), *The Casework Relationship* (London: Allen & Unwin).

Bowers, S. (1949), 'The nature and definition of social casework', *Social Casework*, vol. 30, pp. 311–17, 369–75 and 412–17; reprinted in C. Kasius (ed.), *Principles and Techniques in Social Casework* (Westport: Greenwood Press, 1972).

Brake, M. and Bailey, R. (eds) (1980), *Radical Social Work and Practice* (London: Edward Arnold).

Brandon, J. and Davies, M. (1979), 'The limits of competence in social work: the assessment of marginal students in social work education', *British Journal of Social Work*, vol. 9, pp. 295–347.

Brearley, C. P. (1982), *Risk and Social Work* (London: Routledge & Kegan Paul).

Breen, Jennifer (1981), 'Anti-social language', *The Times Higher Education Supplement*, 24 July.

British Association of Social Workers (1977), *The Social Work Task* (Birmingham: BASW).

Carew, Robert (1979), 'The place of knowledge in social work activity', *British Journal of Social Work*, vol. 9, pp. 349–64.

Clark, F. W., Arkava, M. L. and Associates (1979), *The Pursuit of Competence in Social Work* (San Francisco: Josey Bass).

Cohen, S. (1975), 'It's all right for you to talk: political and sociological manifestos for action', in R. Bailey and M. Brake (eds), *Radical Social Work* (London: Edward Arnold).

Coser, L. A. (ed.) (1963) *Sociology through Literature: An Introductory Reader* (Englewood Cliffs, NJ: Prentice Hall).

Curnock, K. and Hardiker, P. (1979), *Towards Practice Theory: Skills and Methods in Social Assessments* (London: Routledge & Kegan Paul).

Davies, Martin (1981), *The Essential Social Worker: A Guide to Positive Practice* (London: Heinemann Educational).

Day, P. R. (1981), *Social Work and Social Control* (London: Tavistock).

Egan, G. (1975), *The Skilled Helper* (Monterey, EA: Brooks-Cole).

Ferard, M. L. and Hunnybun, N. K. (1962), *The Caseworker's Use of Relationships* (London: Tavistock).

Ford, J. and Hollick, M. (1979), 'The singer or the song: an autobiographical account of a suicidal destructive person and her social worker', *British Journal of Social Work*, vol. 9, pp. 471–88.

Goldstein, H. (1973) *Social Work Practice: A Unitary Approach* (Columbia: University of South Carolina Press).

Gotshalk, D. W. (1962), *Art and the Social Order* (New York: Dover).

Hollis, Florence (1964), *Social Casework: A Psycho-Social Therapy* (New York: Random House)

Home Office (1968), *Report of the Committee on Local Authority and Allied Personal Social Services* (Seebohm Report) (London: HMSO).

Howe, David (1980), 'Inflated states and empty theories in social work', *British Journal of Social Work*, vol. 10, pp. 317–40.

Irvine, E. E. (1969), 'Education for social work: science or humanity', *Social Work*, vol. 26, no. 4, pp. 3–6; reprinted in E. E. Irvine, *Social Work and Human Problems* (Oxford: Pergamon, 1979).

Irvine, E. E. (1974), *Literature and the Study of Human Experience* (Northampton MA: Smith College School for Social Work).

Jehu, Derek (1967), *Learning Theory and Social Work* (London: Routledge & Kegan Paul).

Jones, H. (ed.) (1975), *Towards a New Social Work* (London: Routledge & Kegan Paul).

Jordan, Bill (1978), 'A comment on "Theory and practice in social work"', *British Journal of Social Work*, vol. 8, pp. 23–5.

Jordan, Bill (1979), *Helping in Social Work* (London: Routledge & Kegan Paul).

Katz, Sanford N. (ed.) (1975), *Creativity in Social Work: Selected Writings of Lydia Rapoport* (Philadelphia: Temple Univesity Press).

Kelly, G. A. (1980) *Theory of Personality: Psychology of Personal Constructs* (London: W. W. Norton).

Kermode, Frank (ed.) (1975), *Selected Prose of T. S. Eliot* (London: Faber).

Leavis, F. R. (1962), *The Common Pursuit* (Harmondsworth: Penguin).

Manning, Mary (1980), 'Could the doctors run it better?', *Community Care*, 20 November.

Marris, Peter (1974), *Loss and Change* (London: Routledge & Kegan Paul).

Millard, D. A. (1977), 'Literature and the therapeutic imagination', *British Journal of Social Work*, vol. 7, pp. 173–84.

Ministry of Health, Department of Health for Scotland (1959), *Report of the Working Party on Social Workers in the Local Authority Health and Welfare Services* (The Younghusband Report) (London: HMSO).

Moore, S. (1975), 'Concepts and exercises in the classroom use of Canadian literature', *Canadian Journal of Social Work Education*, vol. 2, pp. 3–11.

Morris, Clare (ed.) (1975), *Literature and the Social Worker: A Reading List for Practitioners, Teachers, Students and Voluntary Workers* (The Library Association).

National Institute for Social Work (1982), *Social Workers: Their Role and Tasks* (The Barclay Report) (London: Bedford Square Press).

O'Hagan, Kieran (1981), 'After the books and essays – coping with others' problems', *Social Work Today*, vol. 12, 3 February, pp. 10–12.

Open University (1971), *Introduction to Art* (Humanities: A Foundation Course, Units 11–12. Prepared by Aaron Scharf and Tim Benton for the Arts Foundation Course Team) (Milton Keynes: Open University Press).

Parad, H. J. (1965), *Crisis Intervention: Selected Readings* (New York: Family Service Association of America).

Parsloe, P. (1972), 'Through the eyes of the probation officer', *British Journal of Social Work*, vol. 2, pp. 21–6.

Picardie, M. (1980), 'Dreadful moments: existential thoughts on doing social work', *British Journal of Social Work*, vol. 10, pp. 483–90.

Pincus, A. and Minahan, A. (1973), *Social Work Practice: Model and Method* (Itasca, IL: Peacock).

Plant, R. (1970), *Social and Moral Theory in Casework* (London: Routledge & Kegan Paul).

Priestley, Philip, *et al.* (1978), *Social Skills and Personal Problem Solving: A Handbook of Methods* (London: Tavistock).

Prins, H. (1974) 'Motivation in social work', *Social Work Today*, vol. 5, pp. 40–3.

Rapoport, Lydia (1960), 'In defense of social work: an examination of stress in the profession', *Social Services Review*, vol. 34, pp. 62–74; reprinted in Katz (1975).

Rapoport, Lydia (1968), 'Creativity in social work', *Smith College Studies in Social Work*, vol. 38, pp. 139–61; reprinted in Katz (1975).

Rayner, P. (1977), 'Psychodrama as a medium for intermediate treatment', *British Journal of Social Work*, vol. 7, pp. 443–53.

Reid, W. and Epstein, L. (1972), *Task-Centred Casework* (New York: Columbia University Press).

Richan, W. and Mendelsohn, A. (1973), *Social Work: The Unloved Profession*, (New York: New Viewpoints).

Rickman, H. P. (1967), *Understanding and the Human Studies* (London: Heinemann Educational).

Rogers, Carl (1969), *On Becoming a Person* (London: Constable).

Ross, B. and Khinduka, S. K. (eds) (1976), *Social Work in Practice: Fourth NASW Symposium* (New York: National Association of Social Workers).

Seligman, M. E. P. (1975), *Helplessness* (San Francisco: Freeman).

Sheldon, Brian (1978), 'Theory and practice in social work: a re-examination of a tenuous relationship', *British Journal of Social Work*, vol. 8, pp. 1–22.

Sheridan, M. (1975), *Children's Developmental Progress from Birth to Five Years: The Stycar Sequences*, 3rd edition (Windsor: National Foundation for Educational Research).

Solomon, B. B. (1976), 'The future of social work skill', in Ross and Khinduka (1976).

Timms, Noel (1971), '. . . *and* Renoir *and* Matisse *and* . . .', An Inaugural Lecture, University of Bradford.

Timms, Noel, and Timms, Rita (1977), *Perspectives in Social Work* (London: Routledge & Kegan Paul).

Totman, R. G. (1979), *Social Causes of Illness* (London: Souvenir Press).

Traux, C. B., and Carkhuff, R. R. (1967), *Towards Effective Counselling and Psychotherapy* (Chicago: Aldine).

Tropp, Emanuel (1976), 'The challenge of quality for practice theory', in Ross and Khinduka (1976).

Valk, M. (1979a), 'The therapeutic imagination: a comment', *British Journal of Social Work*, vol. 9, pp. 87–91.

Valk, M. (1979b), 'Poetry can help: the work of Kenneth Koch', *British Journal of Social Work*, vol. 9, pp. 501–7.

Wellek, R. and Warren, A. (1970), *Theory of Literature*, 3rd edition (New York: Harcourt Brace and World).

Whan, M. W. (1979), 'Accounts, narrative and case history', *British Journal of Social Work*, vol. 9, pp. 489–99.

Wiegand, C. (1979), 'Using a social competence framework for both client and practitioner', in Clark, Arkava and Associates (1979).

Williams, Raymond (1965), *The Long Revolution* (Harmondsworth: Penguin).

Wootton, Barbara (1959), 'Daddy knows best', *Twentieth Century*, vol. 166, pp. 248–61.
Zastrow, C. and Navarre, R. (1979), 'Using video taped role playing to assess and develop competence', in Clark, Arkava and Associates (1979).

Index